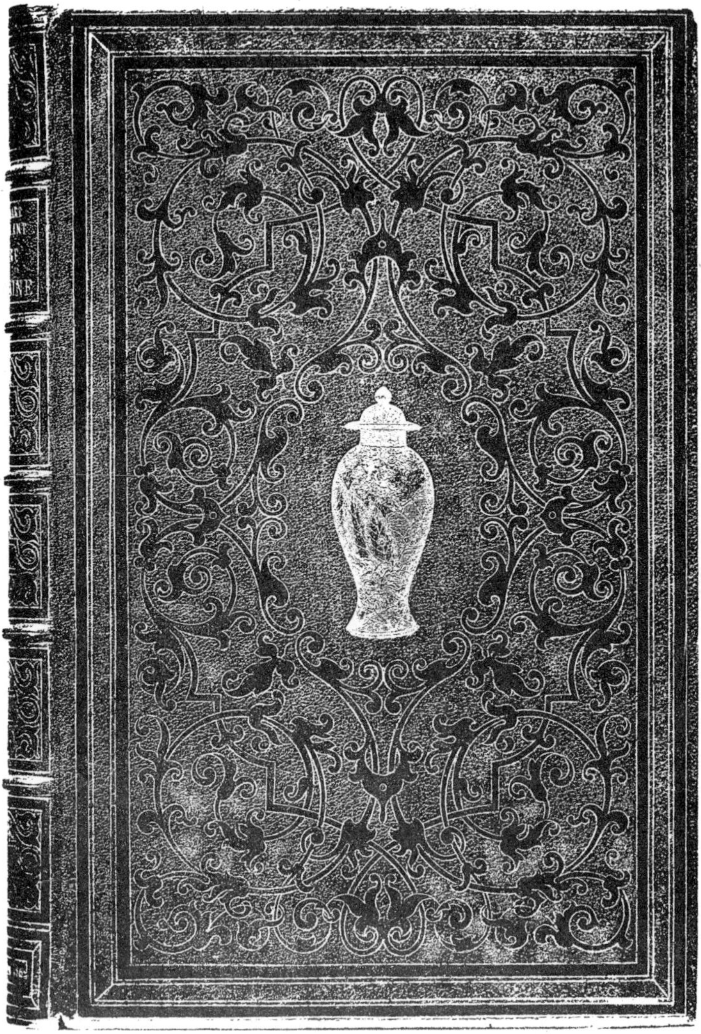

FLORENTINE.

Small folio

The Art of Bookbinding

The Classic Victorian Handbook

JOSEPH W. ZAEHNSDORF

Second Edition, Revised and Enlarged

ILLUSTRATED

DOVER PUBLICATIONS, INC.
Mineola, New York

Bibliographical Note

This Dover edition, first published in 2007, is an unabridged republication of the revised and enlarged second edition of the work originally published in 1890 by George Bell & Sons, London, under the title *The Art of Bookbinding: A Practical Treatise.* The only significant alteration consists in reproducing in black and white the eight plates that had been color-tinted in the original edition.

Library of Congress Cataloging-in-Publication Data

Zaehnsdorf, Joseph William, 1853–1930.
The art of bookbinding : the classic Victorian handbook / Joseph W. Zaehnsdorf.—2nd ed., Rev. and enlarged.
p. cm.
Republication of the revised and enlarged 2nd edition, published by Gregg in 1967, of the work originally published in 1890 by George Bell & Sons, London.
Includes index.
ISBN 0-486-45733-8 (pbk.)
1. Bookbinding—Handbooks, manuals, etc. I. Title.

Z271.Z17 2007
686.3—dc22

2006053478

Manufactured in the United States of America
Dover Publications, Inc., 31 East 2nd Street, Mineola, N.Y. 11501

DEDICATED TO

HUGH OWEN, ESQ., F.S.A.,

AS A SLIGHT ACKNOWLEDGMENT OF HIS COUNSEL AND FRIENDSHIP, AND IN ADMIRATION OF HIS KNOWLEDGE OF

BOOKBINDING.

PREFACE TO THE SECOND EDITION.

THE first edition of this book was written for the use of amateurs, but I found that amongst the members of the trade my little volume had a large sale, and in a short time the edition became exhausted. Repeated applications for the book have induced me to issue this second edition. I have adhered to the arrangement of the first, but a great deal of fresh matter has been added, which I trust will be found useful. Should any of my fellow-workmen find anything new to them I shall be satisfied, knowing that I have done my duty in spreading such knowledge as may contribute towards the advancement of the beautiful art of bookbinding.

I have to record my obligations to those gentlemen who have assisted me by courteously describing the various machines of their invention with which the book is illustrated. The object, however, of illustrating this work with engravings of machines is simply to recognize the fact that books are bound by machinery. To a mechanical worker must be left the task of describing the processes used in this method.

LIST OF PLATES.

CONTENTS.

PART I.—FORWARDING.

PART II.—FINISHING.

GENERAL INFORMATION.

INTRODUCTION.

BOOKBINDING carries us back to the time when leaden tablets with inscribed hieroglyphics were fastened together with rings, which formed what to us would be the binding of the volumes. We might go even still further back, when tiles of baked clay with cuneiform characters were incased one within the other, so that if the cover of one were broken or otherwise damaged there still remained another, and yet another covering; by which care history has been handed down from generation to generation. The binding in the former would consist of the rings which bound the leaden tablets together, and in the latter, the simple covering formed the binding which preserved the contents.

We must pass on from these, and make another pause, when vellum strips were attached together in one continuous length with a roller at each end. The reader unrolled the one, and rolled the other as he perused the work. Books, prized either for their rarity, sacred character, or costliness, would be kept in a round box or case, so that the appearance of a library in Ancient Jerusalem would seem to us as if it were a collection of canisters. The next step was the fastening of separate leaves together, thus making a back, and covering the whole as a protection in a most simple form; the only object being to keep the several leaves in connected sequence. I believe the most ancient form of books formed of separate leaves, will be found in the sacred books of Ceylon which were formed of palm leaves, written on with a metal style, and the binding was merely a silken string tied through one end so loosely as to admit of each leaf being laid down flat when turned over. When the mode of preserving MS. on animal membrane or vellum in separate leaves came into use, the binding was at first only a simple piece of leather wrapped round the book and tied with a thong. These books were not kept on their edges, but were laid down flat on the shelves, and had small cedar tablets hanging from them upon which their titles were inscribed.

The ordinary books for general use were only fastened strongly at the back, with wooden boards for the sides, and simply a piece of leather up the back.

In the sixth century, bookbinding had already taken its place as an "Art," for we have the "Byzantine coatings," as they are called. They are of metal, gold, silver or copper gilt, and sometimes they are enriched with precious stones. The monks, during this century, took advantage of the immense thickness of the wooden boards and frequently hollowed them out to secrete their relics in the cavities. Bookbinding was then confined entirely to the monks who were the literati of the period. Then the art was neglected for some centuries, owing to the plunder and pillage that overran Europe, and books were destroyed to get at the jewels that were supposed to be hidden in the different parts of the covering, so that few now remain to show how bookbinding was then accomplished and to what extent.

We must now pass on to the middle ages, when samples of binding were brought from the East by the crusaders, and these may well be prized by their owners for their delicacy of finish. The monks, who still held the Art of Bookbinding in their hands, improved upon these Eastern specimens. Each one devoted himself to a different branch: one planed the oaken boards to a proper size, another stretched and coloured the leather; and the work was thus divided into branches, as it is now. The task was one of great difficulty, seeing how rude were the implements then in use.

The art of printing gave new life to our trade, and, during the fifteenth century bookbinding made great

Monastic.

progress on account of the greater facility and cheapness with which books were produced. The printer was then his own binder; but as books increased in number, bookbinding became a separate art-trade of itself. This was a step decidedly in the right direction. The art improved so much, that in the sixteenth century some of the finest samples of bookbinding were executed. Morocco having been introduced, and fine delicate tools cut, the art was encouraged by great families, who, liking the Venetian patterns, had their books bound in that style. The annexed woodcut will give a fair idea of a Venetian tool. During this period the French had bookbinding almost entirely in their hands, and Mons. Grolier, who loved the art, had his books bound under his own supervision in the most costly manner. His designs consisted of bold gold lines arranged geometrically with great accuracy, crossing one another and intermixed with small leaves or sprays. These were in outlines shaded or filled up with closely worked cross lines.

Venetian.

Not, however, satisfied with these simple traceries, he embellished them still more by staining or painting them black, green, red, and even with silver, so that they formed bands interlacing each other in a most graceful manner. Opposite is a centre block of Grolier. It will be seen how these lines entwine, and how the small tools are shaded with lines. If the reader has had the good fortune to see one of these specimens, has he not wondered at the taste displayed? To the French must certainly be given the honour of bringing the art to such a perfection. Francis I. and the succeeding monarchs, with the French nobility,

GROLIER.

Royal folio

placed the art on such a high eminence, that even now we are compelled to look to these great masterpieces as models of style. Not only was the exterior elaborate in ornament, but the edges were gilded and tooled; and even painted. We must wonder at the excellence of the materials and the careful workmanship which has preserved the bindings, even to the colour of the leather, in perfect condition to the present day.

Grolier.

There is little doubt that the first examples of the style now known as "*Grolier*" were produced in Venice, under the eye of Grolier himself, and according to his own designs; and that workmen in France, soon rivalled and excelled the early attempts. The work of Maioli may be distinctly traced by the bold simplicity and purity of his designs; and more especially by the broader gold lines which margin the coloured bands of geometric and arabesque ornamentation.

All books, it must be understood, were not bound in so costly a manner, for we find pigskin, vellum and calf in use. The latter was especially preferred on account of its peculiar softness, smooth surface, and great aptitude for receiving impressions of dumb or blind tooling. It was only towards the latter part of the sixteenth century that the English binders began to employ delicate or fine tooling.

During the seventeenth century the names of Du Sueil and Le Gascon were known for the delicacy and extreme minuteness of their finishing. Not disdaining the bindings of the Italian school, they took from them new ideas; for whilst the Grolier bindings were bold, the Du Sueil and Le Gascon more resembled fine lace work of intricate design, with harmonizing flowers and other objects, from which we may obtain a great variety of artistic character. During this period embroidered velvet was much in use. Then a change took place and a style was adopted which by some people would be preferred to the gorgeous bindings of the sixteenth century. The sides were finished quite plainly with only a line round the edge of the boards (and in some instances not even that) with a coat of arms or some badge in the centre.

Towards the end of the seventeenth century bookbinding began to improve, particularly with regard to forwarding. The joints were true and square, and the back was made to open more freely. In the eighteenth century the names of Derome, Roger Payne, and others are prominent as masters of the craft, and the Harleian style was introduced.

The plate facing may be fairly estimated as a good specimen of Derome. Notice the extreme simplicity and yet the symmetry of the design; its characteristic feature being the boldness of the corners and the gradual diminishing of the scroll work as it nears the centre of the panel. Morocco and calf were the leathers used for this binding.

Hand coloured calf was at this period at its height, and

GASCON.

8vo

the Cambridge calf may be named as a pattern of one of the various styles, and one that is approved of by many at the present day—the calf was sprinkled all over, save a square panel left uncoloured in the centre of the boards.

The Harleian style took its name from Harley, Earl of Oxford. It was red morocco with a broad tooled border and centre panels. We have the names of various masters who pushed the art forward to very great excellence during this century. Baumgarten and Benedict, two Germans of

Harleian.

considerable note in London; Mackinly, from whose house also fine work was sent out, and by whom good workmen were educated whose specimens almost equal the work of their master. There were two other Germans, Kalthoeber and Staggemeier, each having his own peculiar style. Kalthoeber is credited with having first introduced painting on the edges. This I must dispute, as it was done in the sixteenth century. To him, however, must certainly be given the credit of having discovered the secret, if ever lost, and renewing it on his best work. We must now pass on to Roger Payne, that unfortunate and erring man but clever workman, who lived during the latter part of the eighteenth century. His taste may be seen from the woodcut. He generally used small tools, and by combining them formed a variety of beautiful designs. He cut most of these tools himself, either because he could not find a tool cutter of sufficient skill, or that he found it difficult to

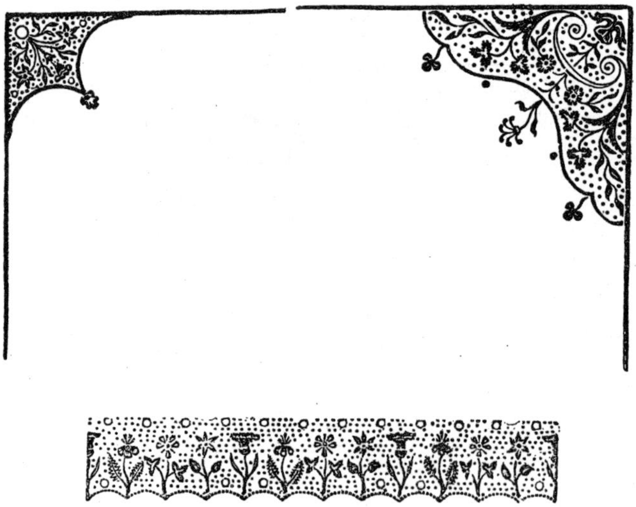

Roger Payne.

pay the cost. We are told by anecdote, that he drank much and lived recklessly; but notwithstanding all his irregular habits, his name ought to be respected for the work he executed. His backs were firm, and his forwarding excellent; and he introduced a class of finishing that was always in accordance with the character or subject of the book. His only fault was the peculiar coloured paper with which he made his end papers.

Coloured or fancy calf has now taken the place of the hand-coloured. Coloured cloth has come so much into use, that this branch of the trade alone monopolizes nearly three-fourths of the workmen and females employed in bookbinding. Many other substitutes for leather have been introduced, and a number of imitations of morocco and calf are in the market; this, with the use of machinery, has made so great a revolution in the trade, that it is now divided into two distinct branches—cloth work and extra work.

I have endeavoured in the foregoing remarks to raise the emulation of my fellow craftsmen by naming the most famous artists of past days; men whose works are most worthy of study and imitation. I have refrained from any notice or criticism of the work of my contemporaries; but I may venture to assure the lover of good bookbinding that as good and sound work, and as careful finish, may be obtained in a first-rate house in London as in any city in the world.

In the succeeding chapters, I will endeavour in as plain and simple a way as I can to give instructions to the unskilled workman *how to bind a book*.

PART I.

FORWARDING.

THE ART OF BOOKBINDING.

CHAPTER I.

Folding.

We commence with *folding*. It is generally the first thing the binder has to do with a book. The sheets are either supplied by the publisher or printer (mostly the printer); should the amateur wish to have his books in sheets, he may generally get them by asking his bookseller for them. It is necessary that they be carefully folded, for unless they are perfectly even, it is impossible that the margins (the blank space round the print) can be uniform when the book is cut. Where the margin is small, as in very small prayer books, a very great risk of cutting into the print is incurred; besides, it is rather annoying to see a book which has the folio or paging on one leaf nearly at the top, and on the next, the print touching the bottom; to remedy such an evil, the printer having done his duty by placing his margins quite true, it remains with the binder to perfect and bring the sheet into proper form by folding. The best bound book may be spoilt by having the sheets badly folded, and the binder is perfectly justified in rejecting any sheets that may be badly printed, that is, not in register.

The sheets are laid upon a table with the signatures (the letters or numbers that are at the foot of the first page of each sheet when folded) facing downwards on the left hand side. A folding-stick is held in the right hand, and the sheet is brought over from right to left, the folios being carefully placed together; if the paper is held up to the light, and is not too thick, it can be easily seen through. Holding the two together and laying them on the table the folder is drawn across the sheet, creasing the centre; then, holding the sheet down with the folder on the line to be creased, the top part is brought over and downwards till the folios or the bottom of the letterpress or print is again even. The folder is then drawn across, and so by bringing each folio together the sheet is completed. The process is extremely simple. The octavo sheet is *generally* folded into 4 folds, thus giving 8 leaves or 16 pages; a quarto, into 2, giving 4 leaves or 8 pages, and the sheets properly folded, will have *their signatures outside* at the foot of the first page. If the signature is not on the outside, one may be certain that the sheet has been wrongly folded.

I say *generally;* at one time the water or wire mark on the paper and the number of folds gave the size of the book.

There are numerous other sizes, but it is not necessary to give them all; the process of folding is in nearly all cases the same; here are however, a few of the sizes given in inches.

Foolscap 8vo.	$6\frac{5}{8} \times 4\frac{1}{8}$
Demy 12mo.	$7\frac{3}{8} \times 4\frac{3}{8}$
Crown 8vo.	$7\frac{1}{2} \times 5$
Post 8vo.	8×5
Demy 8vo.	$9 \times 5\frac{1}{2}$
Medium 8vo.	$9\frac{5}{8} \times 5\frac{3}{4}$
Small Royal 8vo.	$10 \times 6\frac{1}{4}$
Large Royal 8vo.	$10\frac{1}{2} \times 6\frac{3}{4}$

Imperial 8vo.	$11 \times 7\frac{1}{2}$
Demy 4to.	11×9
Medium 4to.	$11\frac{3}{4} \times 9\frac{5}{8}$
Royal 4to.	$12\frac{1}{2} \times 10$
Imperial 4to.	15×11
Crown Folio.	15×10
Demy Folio	18×11

As a final caution, the first and last sheets must be carefully examined; very often the sheet has to be cut up or divided, and the leaf or leaves placed in various positions in the book.

It is also advisable to cut the head of the sheets, using the folding-stick, cutting just beyond the back or middle fold; this prevents the sheet running into a side crease when pressing or rolling. Should such a crease occur the leaf or sheet must be damped by placing it between wet paper and subjecting it to pressure; no other method is likely to erase the break.

Refolding.—With regard to books that have been issued in numbers, they must be *pulled to pieces* or divided. The parts being arranged in consecutive order, so that not so much difficulty will be felt in collating the sheets, the outside wrapper is torn away, and each sheet pulled singly from its neighbour, care being taken to see if any thread used in sewing is in the centre of the sheet at the back; if so, it must be cut with a knife or it will tear the paper. As the sheets are pulled they must be laid on the left hand side, each sheet being placed face downwards; should they be placed face upwards the first sheet will be the last and the whole will require rearranging. All advertisements may be placed away from the sheets into a pile; these will be found very handy for lining boards, pasting on, or as waste. The title and contents will generally be found in the last part; place them in their proper places. The sheets must now be refolded, if improperly folded in the first instance.

Turn the whole pile (or book now) over, and again go through each sheet; alter by refolding any sheet that may require it. Very often the sheets are already cut, and in this case the section must be dissected and each leaf refolded and reinserted in proper sequence, and placed carefully head-line to head-line. Great care must be exercised, as the previous creasings render the paper liable to be torn in the process.

Books that have been bound and cut would be rendered often worse by refolding, and as a general rule they are left alone. Bound books are pulled to pieces in the same manner, always taking care that the thread is cut or

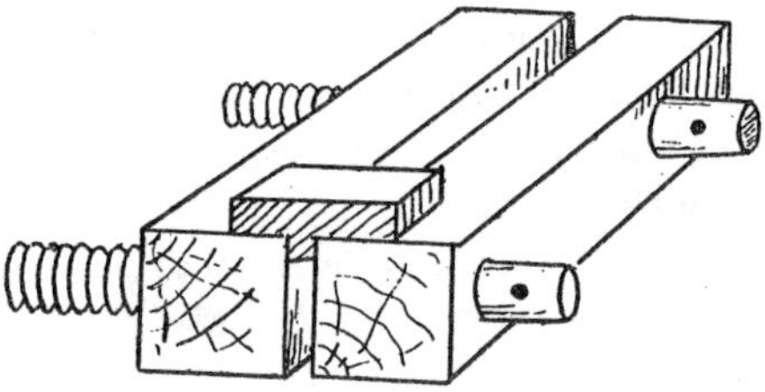

Knocking-down Iron screwed into Press.

loose before tearing the sheet away; should trouble arise through the glue, etc., not coming away easily, the back may be damped with a sponge lightly charged with water, or perhaps a better method is to place the book or books in a press, screw up tightly, and soak the backs with thin paste, leaving them soaking for an hour or two; they will want repasting two or three times during the period; the whole of the paper, glue, and leather can then be easily scraped away with a blunt knife; a handful of shavings rubbed over the back will make it quite clean, and no difficulty will be met with if the sections are taken apart while damp. The sections must, as pulled, be placed evenly one on the other, as the paper at back retains sufficient glue to cause them to stick together if laid across one another; the whole must then be left to dry. When dry the groove should be knocked down on a flat surface, and for this the knocking-down iron screwed up in the lying press is perhaps the best thing to use. The groove is the projecting part of the

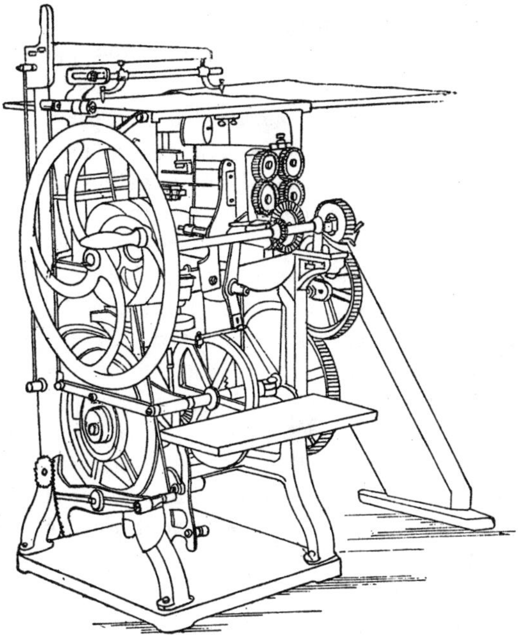

Martini's Folding Machine.

book close to the back, caused by the backing, and is the groove for the back edge of the mill-board to work in by a hinge; this hinge is technically called the "joint."

Machines.—There are many folding machines made by the various machinists; the working of them, however, is in nearly all cases identical. The machine is generally fed by a girl, who places the sheet to points, the arm lifting up at given periods to allow placing the sheet. Another arm carrying a long thin blade descends, taking the sheet through a slot in the table, where it is passed between rollers; another set of rollers at right angles creases it again. The rollers are arranged for two, three, or more creasings or folds. The sheets are delivered at the side into a box, from which they are taken from time to time. The cut is one of Martini's, and is probably the most advanced.

Gathering.—A *gathering machine* has been patented which is of a simple but ingenious contrivance for the quick gathering of sheets. The usual way to gather, is by laying piles of sheets upon a long table, and for the gatherer to take from each pile a sheet in succession. By the new method a round table is made to revolve by machinery, and upon it are placed the piles of sheets. As the table revolves the gatherer takes a sheet from each pile as it passes him. It will at once be seen that not only is space saved, but that a number of gatherers may be placed at the table; and that there is no possibility of the gatherers shirking their work, as the machine is made to register the revolutions. By comparing the number of sheets with the revolutions of the table, the amount of work done can be checked.

CHAPTER II.

BEATING AND ROLLING.

THE object of beating or rolling is to make the book as solid as possible. For beating, a stone or iron slab, used as a bed, and a heavy hammer, are necessary. The stone or iron must be perfectly smooth, and should be bedded with great solidity. I have in use an iron bed about two feet square, fitted into a strongly-made box, filled with sand, with a wooden cover to the iron when not in use. The hammer should be somewhat bell-shaped, and weigh about ten pounds, with a short handle, made to *fit the hand.* The face of the hammer and stone (it is called a beating-stone whether it be stone or iron), must be kept perfectly clean, and it is advisable always to have a piece of paper at the top and bottom of the sections when beating, or the repeated concussion will glaze them.

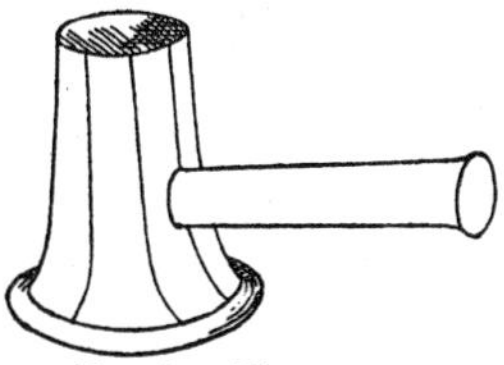

Beating Hammer.

The book should be divided into lots or sections of about half an inch thick, that will be about fifteen to twenty sheets, according to the thickness of paper. A section is now to be held on the stone between the fingers and thumb of the left hand; then the hammer, grasped firmly in the right hand, is raised, and brought down with rather more than its own weight on the sheets, which must be continually moved round, turned over and changed about, in order that they may be equally beaten all over.

By passing the section between the finger and thumb, it can be felt at once, if it has been beaten properly and evenly. Great care must be taken that in each blow of the hammer it shall have the face fairly on the body of the section, for if the hammer is so used that the greatest portion of the weight should fall outside the edge of the sheets the concussion will break away the paper as if cut with a knife. It is perhaps better for a beginner to practise on some waste paper before attempting to beat a book; and he should always rest when the wrist becomes tired. When each section has been beaten, supposing a book has been divided into four sections, the whole four should be beaten again, but together.

I do not profess a preference to beating over rolling because I have placed it first. The rolling machine is one of the greatest improvements in the trade, but *all books should not be rolled*, and a bookbinder, I mean a practical bookbinder, not one who has been nearly the whole of his lifetime upon a cutting machine, or at a blocking press, and who calls himself one, but a competent bookbinder, should know how and when to use the beating hammer and when the rolling machine.

There are some books, old ones for instance, that should on no account be rolled. The clumsy presses used in printing at an early date gave such an amount of pressure on the type that the paper round their margins has sometimes two or three times the thickness of the printed portion. At the present time each sheet after having been printed is pressed, and thus the leaf is made flat or nearly so, and for such work the rolling machine is certainly better than the hammer.

To roll a book, it is divided into sections as in beating, only not so many sheets are taken—from six upwards, according to the quality of the work to be executed. The sheets are then placed between tins, and the whole passed between the rollers, which are regulated by a screw, according to the thickness of sections and power required. The workman, technically called "Roller," has to be very careful in passing his books through, that his hand be not drawn in as well, for accidents have from time to time occurred through the inattention of the Roller

Rolling Machine.

himself, or of the individual who has the pleasure of applying his strength to turning the handle.

I never pass or hear a rolling machine revolving very rapidly without having vividly brought to my mind a very serious accident that happened to my father. He was feeling for a flaw on one of the rollers, and whilst his hands were at the edge of the rollers the man turned the handle, drawing the whole hand between the heavy cylinders. The accident cost him many months in the hospital, and he never regained complete use of his right hand.

Great care must be used not to pass too many sheets through the machine at one time; the same applies to the regulating screw. The amount of damage that can be done to the paper by too heavy a pressure is astonishing, as the paper becomes quite brittle, and may perhaps even be cut as with a knife.

Another caution respecting new work. Recently printed books, if submitted to heavy pressure, either by the beating hammer or machine, are very likely to "set off," that is, the ink from one side of the page will be imprinted to its opposite neighbour; indeed, under very heavy pressure, some ink, perhaps many years old, will "set off;" this is due in a great measure to the ink not being properly prepared.

Machines.—Of the many rolling machines in the market the principle is in all the same. A powerful frame, carrying two heavy rollers or cylinders, which are set in motion, revolving in the same direction, by means of steam or by hand. In many, extra power is supplied by the use of extra cog-wheels; the power is, however, gained at an expense of speed. The pressure is regulated by screws at the top.

CHAPTER III.

Collating.

To collate, is to ensure that each sheet or leaf is in its proper sequence. Putting the sheets together and placing plates or maps requires great attention. The sheets must run in proper order by the signatures: letters are mostly used, but numbers are sometimes substituted. When letters are used, the alphabet is repeated as often as necessary, doubling the letter as often as a new alphabet is used, as B, C, with the first alphabet,[1] and AA, BB, CC or Aa, Bb, Cc, with the second repetition, and three letters with the third, generally leaving out J, V, W. Plates must be trimmed or cut to the proper size before being placed in the book, and maps that are to be folded must be put on guards. By mounting a map on a guard the size of the page, it may be kept open on the table beside the book, which may be opened at any part without concealing the map: by this method the map will remain convenient for constant reference. This is technically called "throwing out" a map.

To collate a book, it is to be held in the right hand, at the right top corner, then, with a turn of the wrist, the back must be brought to the front. Fan the sections out, then with the left hand the sheets must be brought back to an angle, which will cause them when released to spring forward, so that the letter on the right bottom

[1] The text of a book always commences with B, the title and preliminary matter being reckoned as A.

corner of each sheet is seen, and then released, and the next brought into view. When a work is completed in more than one volume, the number of the volume is indicated at the left hand bottom corner of each sheet. I need hardly mention that the title should come first, then the dedication (if one), preface, contents, then the text, and finally the index. The number on the pages will, however, always direct the binder as to the placing of the sheets. The book should always be beaten or rolled before placing plates or maps, *especially coloured ones.*

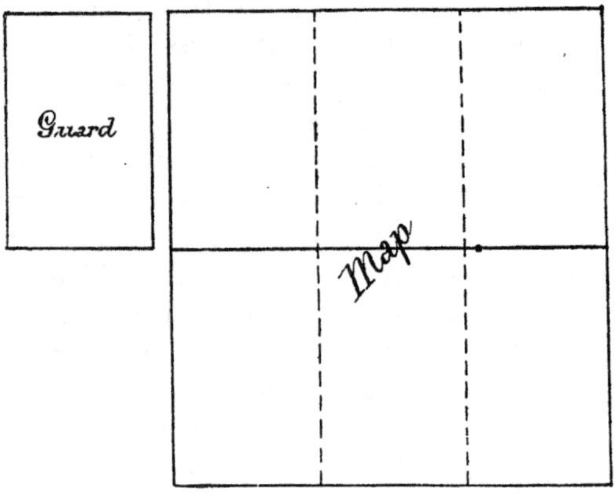

Presuming that we have a book with half a dozen plates, the first thing after ascertaining that the letter-press is perfect, is to see that all the plates are there, by looking to the "List of Plates," printed generally after the contents. The plates should then be squared or cut truly, using a sharp knife and straight edge. When the plates are printed on paper larger than the book, they must be cut down to the proper size, leaving a somewhat less margin at the back than there will be at the foredge when the book is cut. Some plates have to face to the left, some to the right, the frontispiece for instance; but as a general rule, plates should be placed on the right hand, so that on opening the book they all face upwards. When plates consist of subjects that are at a right angle with the text, such as views and landscapes, the inscription should always be placed to the right hand, whether the plate face to the right or to the left page. If the plates are on thick paper they should be *guarded*, either by adding a piece of paper of the same thickness or by cutting a piece from the plate and then joining the two again together with a piece of linen, so that the plate moves on the linen hinge: the space between the guard and plate should be more than equal to the thickness of the paper. If the plate is almost a cardboard, it is better and stronger if linen be placed both back and front. Should the book consist of plates only, sections may be made by placing two plates and two guards together, and sewing through the centre between the guards, leaving of course a space between the two guards, which will form the back.

With regard to maps that have to be mounted, it is better to mount them on the finest linen, as it takes up the least room in the thickness of the book. The linen should be cut a little larger than the map itself, with a further piece left, on which to mount the extra piece of paper, so that the map may be thrown out as before described. The map should first be trimmed at its back, then pasted with rather *thin paste;* the linen should then be laid carefully on, and gently rubbed down and turned over, so that the map comes uppermost; the pasted guard should then be placed a little away from the map, and the whole *well rubbed down*, and finally laid out flat to dry. To do this work, the paste must be clean, free from all lumps, and used very evenly and not too thickly, or when dry every mark of the brush will be visible. When the map is dry it should be trimmed all round and folded to its proper size, viz.—a trifle smaller than the book will be when cut. If it is left larger the folds will naturally be cut away, and the only remedy will be a new map, which means a new copy of the work. For all folded maps or plates a corresponding thickness must be placed in the backs where the maps go, or the foredge will be thicker than the back. Pieces of paper called guards, are folded from $\frac{1}{4}$ inch to 1 inch in width, according to the size of the book, and placed in the back, and sewn through as a section. Great care must be taken that these guards are not folded too large, so as to overlap the folds of the map, if they do so, the object of their being placed there to make the thickness of the back and foredge equal will be defeated.

Shewing Book with Map thrown out.

In a great measure, the whole beauty of the inside work rests in properly collating the book, in guarding maps, and in placing the plates. When pasting in any single leaves or plates, a piece of waste paper should always be placed on the leaf or plate the required distance from the edge to be pasted, so that the leaf is pasted straight. It takes no longer to lay the plate down upon the edge of a board with a paper on the plate, than it does to hold the plate in the left hand, and apply the paste with the right hand middle finger; by the former method a proper amount of paste is deposited evenly on the plate and it is pasted in a straight line; by the latter method, it is pasted in some places thickly, and in some places none at all. I have often seen books with the plates fastened to the book nearly half way up to its foredge, and thus spoilt, only through the slovenly way of pasting. After having placed the plates, the collater should go through them again when dry, to see if they adhere properly, and break or fold them over up to the pasting, with a folding stick, so that they will lie flat when the book is open. I must again call attention to coloured plates. They should be looked to during the whole of binding, especially after pressing. The amount of gum that is put on the surface, which is very easily seen by the gloss, causes them to stick to the letter-press: should they so stick, do not try to tear them apart, but warm a polishing iron and pass it over the plate and letter-press, placing a piece of paper between the iron and the book to avoid dirt. The heat and moisture will soften the gum, and the surfaces can then be very easily separated. By rubbing a little *powdered French chalk* over the coloured plates *before* sticking them in, these *ill effects will be avoided.*

It sometimes happens that the whole of a book is composed of single leaves, as the "Art Journal." Such a book should be collated properly, and the plates placed to their respective places, squared and broken over, by placing a straight edge or runner about half an inch from its back edge, and running a folder under the plate, thus lifting it to the edge of the runner. The whole book should then be pressed for a few hours, taken out, and the back glued up; the back having been previously roughed with the side edge of the saw. To glue such a back, the book is placed in the lying press between boards, with the back projecting about an eighth of an inch, the saw is then drawn over it, with its side edge, so that the paper is as it were rasped. The back is then sawn in properly, as explained in the next chapter, and the whole back is glued. When dry, the book is separated into divisions or sections of four, six, or eight leaves, according to the thickness of the paper, and each section is then overcast or over sewn along its whole length, the thread being fastened at the head and tail (or top and bottom); thus each section is made independent of its neighbour. The sections should then be gently struck along the back edge with a hammer against a knocking-down iron, so as to imbed the thread into the paper, or the back will be too thick. The thread should not be struck so hard as to cut the paper, or break the thread, but very gently. Two or three sections may be taken at a time.

After having placed the plates, the book should be put into the press (standing or otherwise) for a few hours. A standing press is used in all good bookbinding shops.

The Paris houses have a curious way of pressing their books. The books are placed in the standing press; the top and bottom boards are very thick, having a groove cut in them in which a strong thin rope is placed. The press is screwed down tightly, when, after some few minutes has elapsed, the cord or rope is drawn together and fastened. The pressure of the screw is released, the whole taken out *en bloc*, and allowed to remain for some hours, during which time a number of other batches are passed through the same press.

When taken out of the press the book is ready for "marking up" if for flexible sewing, or for being sawn in if for ordinary work.

Interleaving.—It is sometimes required to place a piece of writing paper between each leaf of letter-press, either for notes or for a translation: in such a case, the book must be properly beaten or rolled, and each leaf cut up with a hand-knife, both head and foredge; the writing paper having been chosen, must be folded to the size of the book and pressed. A single leaf of writing paper is now to be fastened in the centre of each section, and a folded leaf placed to every folded letter-press leaf, by inserting the one within the other, a folded writing paper being left outside every other section, and all being put level with the head; the whole book should then be well pressed.

If by any chance there should be one sheet in duplicate and another missing, by returning the one to the publisher of the book the missing sheet is generally replaced; this, of course, has reference only to books of a recent date.

There is a new press of American invention that has come under my notice. It will be seen that it acts on an entirely new principle, having two horizontal screws instead of one perpendicular. The power is first applied by hand and finally by a lever and ratchet-wheel in the centre. A pressure guage is affixed to each press, so that the actual power exerted may be ascertained as the operation proceeds. The press can be had from Messrs. Ladd and Co., 116, Queen Victoria Street, E.C.; and they claim that it gives a pressure equal to the hydraulic press, without any of the hydraulic complications.

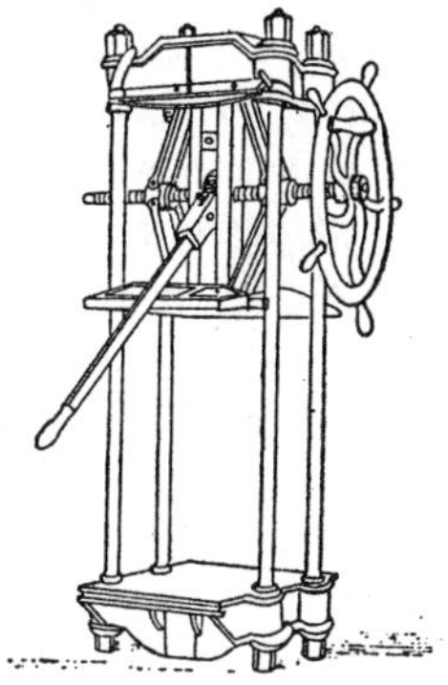

Boomer Press.

CHAPTER IV.

Marking up and Sawing in.

The books having been in the press a sufficient time, say for a night, they are taken out, and run through again (collated) to make sure that they are all correct. A book is then taken and knocked straight both head and back and put in the lying press between boards, projecting from them about $\frac{1}{8}$ inch; some binders prefer cutting boards, I prefer pressing boards, and I should advise the use of them, as the whole can be knocked up together. They should be held between the fingers of each hand, and the back and head knocked alternately on the cheek of the press. The boards are then drawn back the required distance from the back of the book: the book and boards must now be held tightly with the left hand, and the whole carefully lowered into the press; the right hand regulating the screws, which should then be screwed up tightly. The book is now quite straight, and firmly fixed in the press, and we have to decide if it is to be sewn flexibly or not. If for *flexible* binding the book is *not to be sawn in*, but marked; the difference being, that with the latter the cord is *outside the sheets;* with the former the cord is *imbedded in the back*, in the cut or groove made by the saw. We will take the flexible first, and suppose that the book before us is an ordinary 8vo. volume, and that it is to be cut all round.

The back should be divided into six equal portions, leaving the bottom, or tail, half an inch longer than the rest, simply because of a curious optical illusion, by which, if the spaces were all equal in width, the bottom one would appear to be the smallest, although accurately of the same width as the rest. This curious effect may be tested on any framed or mounted print. A square is now to be laid upon the back exactly to the marks, and marked pretty black with a lead pencil; the head and tail must now be sawn in to imbed the chain of the kettle stitch, at a distance sufficient to prevent the thread being divided by accident in cutting. In flexible work great accuracy is absolutely necessary throughout the whole of the work, especially in the marking up, as the form of the bands will be visible when covered. It will be easily seen if the book has been knocked up straight by laying the square at the head when the book is in the press, and if it is not straight, it must be taken out and corrected. If the book is very small, as for instance a small prayer book, it is usually marked up for five bands, but only sewed on three; the other two being fastened on as false bands when the book is ready for covering. There would be no gain in strength by sewing a small book on fine bands.

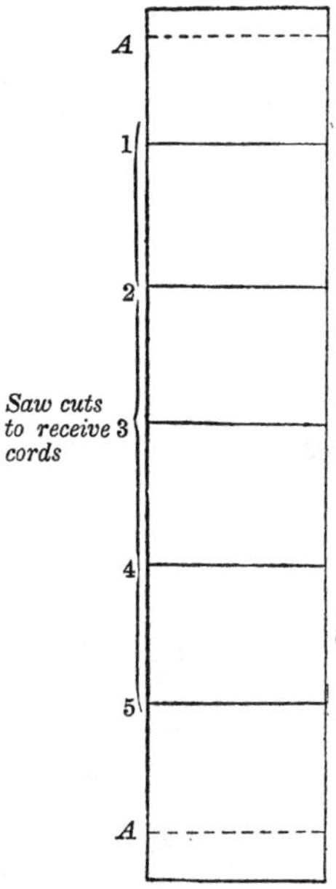

A. Saw marks for catch-up stitch.

When the book is to be "sawn in," it is marked up as for flexible work, but the back is sawn, both for the bands and kettle stitch, with a tennon saw. In choosing the saw, it should be one with the teeth not spread out too much; and it is advisable to have two of different widths. Care must be taken that the saw does not enter too deeply, and one must, in all cases, *be guided in the depth by the thickness of the cord to be used.* The size of the book should determine the thickness of the cord, as the larger the book, the stronger and thicker must be the cord. Suitable cord is to be purchased at all the bookbinder's material shops, and it is known by the size of the book, such as 12mo., 8vo., 4to. cord.

Sawing-in Machine.

I think nothing looks worse than a book with great holes in the back, sometimes to be seen when the book is opened, which are due to the inattention of the workmen. Besides, it causes great inconvenience to the forwarder if the cords are loose, and the only thing he can do in such a case is to cram a lot of glue into the grooves to keep the cord in its place. If, on the other hand, the saw cuts are not deep enough, the cord will stand out from the back, and be distinctly seen when the book is finished, if not remedied by extra strips of leather or paper between the bands when lining up. It is better to use double thin cord instead of one thick one for large books, because the two cords will lie and imbed themselves in the back, whereas one large one will not, unless very deep and wide saw cuts be made. Large folios should be sawn on six or seven bands, but five for an 8vo. is the right number, from which all other sizes can be regulated.

Saw benches have been introduced by various firms. They can be driven either by steam or foot. It will be seen that the saws are circular, and can be shifted on the spindle to suit the various sized books. As the books themselves are slid along the table on the saws, the advantage is very great in a large shop where much work of one size is done at a time.

CHAPTER V.

Sewing.

Flexible Work.—The "sewing press" consists of a *bed, two screws,* and a *beam* or *cross bar,* round which are fastened five or more cords, called *lay cords.* Five pieces of cord cut from the ball, in length, about four times the thickness of the book, are fastened to the lay cords by slip knots; the other ends being fastened to small pieces of metal called *keys,* by twisting the ends round twice and then a half hitch. The keys are then passed through the slot in the bed of the "press," and the beam screwed up rather tightly; but loose enough to allow the lay cords to move freely backwards or forwards. Having the book on the bed of the press with the back towards the sewer, a few sheets (better than only one) are laid against the cords, and they are arranged exactly to the marks made on the back of the sections. When quite true and perpendicular, they should be made tight by screwing the beam up. It will be better if the cords are a little to the right of the press, so that the sewer may get her or his left arm to rest better on the press.

If when the press is tightened one of the cords is loose,

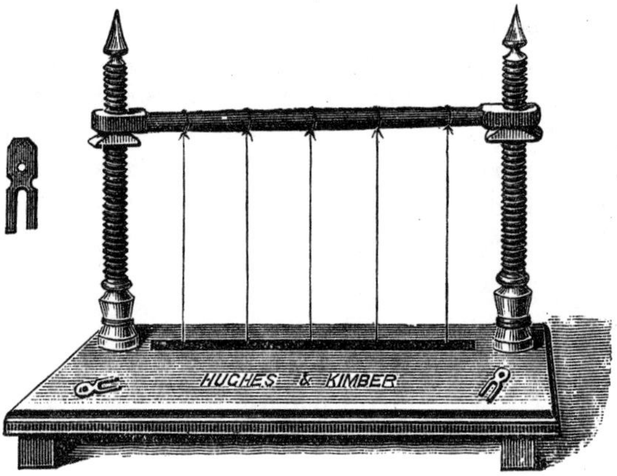

Sewing Press.

as will sometimes happen, a pencil, folding-stick or other object slipped under the lay cord on the top of the beam will tighten the band sufficiently. The foreign sewing presses have screws with a hook at the end to hold the bands, the screws running in a slot in the beam: in practice they are very convenient.

The first and last sections are overcast usually with cotton or very fine thread. The first sheet is now to be laid against the bands, and the needle introduced through the kettle stitch hole on the right of the book, which is the head. The left hand being within the centre of the sheet, the needle is taken with it, and thrust out *on the left* of the mark made for the first band; the needle being taken with the right hand, is again introduced on *the right* of the same band, thus making a *complete circle* round it. This is repeated with each band in succession, and the needle brought out of the kettle stitch hole on the left or tail of the sheet. A new sheet is now placed on the top, and treated in a similar way, by introducing the needle at the left end or tail; and when taken out at the right end or top, the thread must be fastened by a knot to the end, hanging from the first sheet, which is left long enough for the purpose. A third sheet having been sewn in like manner,[1] the needle must be brought out at the kettle stitch, thrust between the two sheets first sewn, and drawn round the thread, thus fastening each sheet to its neighbour by a kind of chain stitch. I believe the term "kettle stitch" is only a corruption of "catch-up stitch," as it catches each section as sewn in succession. This class of work must be done very neatly and evenly, but it is easily done with a little practice and patience. This is the strongest sewing executed at the present day, but it is very seldom done, as it takes three or four times as long as the ordinary sewing. The thread must be drawn tightly each time it is passed round the band, and at the end properly fastened off at the kettle stitch, or the sections will work loose in course of time. Old books were always sewn in this manner, and when two or double bands were used, the thread was twisted twice round one on sewing one section, and twice round the other on sewing the next, or once round each cord. In some cases even the "head-band" was worked at

[1] As each thread is terminated, another must be joined thereto, so that one length of thread is, as it were, used for a book. The knots must be made very neatly, and the ends cut off, or they will be visible in the sheet by their bulk.

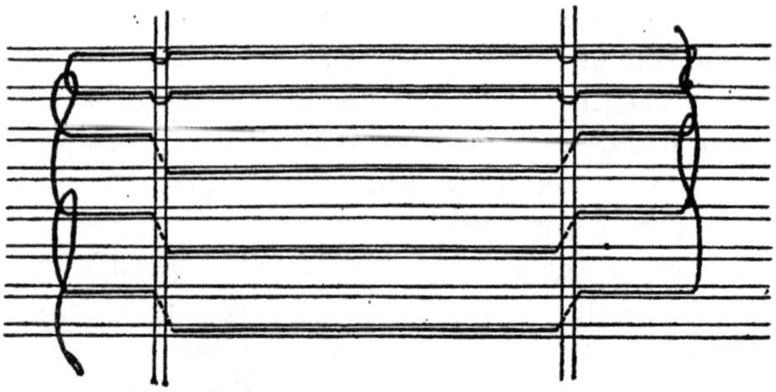

Ordinary sewing. 2 sheets on 2 bands.

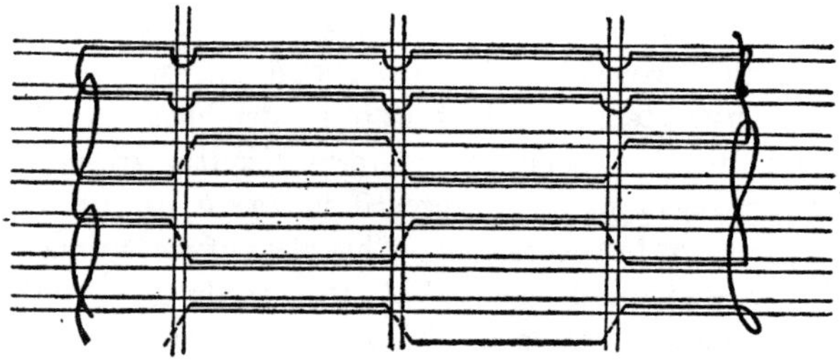

Ordinary sewing. 2 sheets on 3 bands.

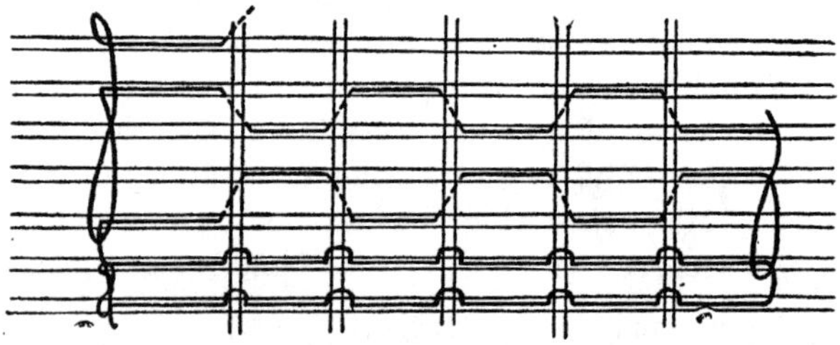

Ordinary sewing. 2 sheets on 5 bands.

The thick lines shewing the direction of the thread.

the same time, by fastening other pieces of leather for the head and tail, and making it the catch-up stitch as well. When the head-band was worked in sewing, the book was, of course, not afterwards cut at the edges. When this was done, wooden boards were used instead of mill boards, and twisted leather instead of cord, and when the book was covered, a groove was made between each double band. This way is still imitated by sticking a second band or cord alongside the one made in sewing, before the book is covered. The cord for flexible work is called a "flexible cord," and is twisted tighter and is stronger than any other. In all kinds of sewing I advise the use of Hayes' Royal Irish thread, not because there is no other of good

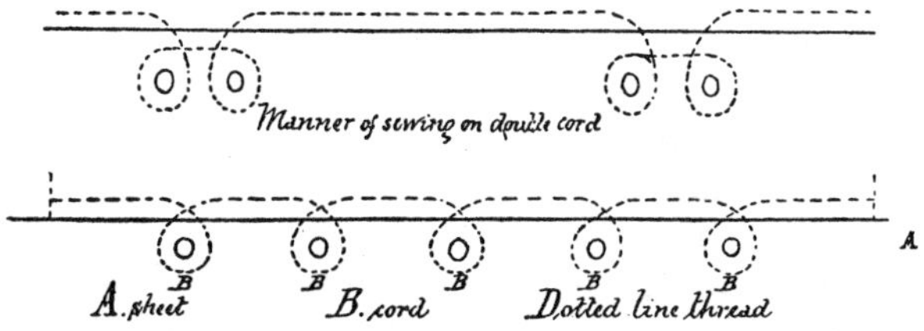

Flexible sewing.

manufacture, but because I have tried several kinds, and Hayes' has proved to be the best. The thickness of the cord must always be in proportion to the size and thickness of the book, and the thickness of the thread must depend on the sheets, whether they be half sheets or whole sheets. If too thick a thread is used, the swelling (the rising caused in the back by the thread) will be too much, and it will be impossible to make a proper rounding or get a right size "groove" in backing. If the sections are thick or few, a thick thread must be used to give the thickness necessary to produce a good groove.

If the book is of moderate thickness, the sections may be knocked down by occasionally tapping them with a piece of wood loaded at one end with lead, or a thick folding-stick may be used as a substitute. I must again call particular attention to the kettle stitch. The thread must not be drawn *too tight* in making the chain, or the thread *will break in backing;* but still a proper tension must be kept or the sheets will wear loose. The last sheet should be fastened with a double knot round the kettle stitch two or three sections down, and that section must be sewn all along. The next style of sewing, and most generally used throughout the trade, is the ordinary method.

Ordinary Sewing is somewhat different, inasmuch as *the thread is not* twisted round the cord, as in flexible work, when the cord is outside the section. In this method the cord fits into the saw cuts. The thread is simply passed over the cord, not round it, otherwise the principle of sewing is the same, that is, the thread is passed right along the section, out of the holes made, and into them again; the kettle stitch being made in the same way. This style of work has one advantage over flexible work, because the back of the book can be better gilt. In flexible work, the leather is attached with paste to the back, and is flexed, and bent, each time the book is opened, and there is great risk of the gold splitting away or being detached from the leather in wear. Books sewn in the ordinary method are made with a hollow or loose back, and when the book is opened, the crease in the back is independent of the leather covering; the lining of the back only is creased, and the leather keeps its perfect form, by reason of the lining giving it a spring outwards. Morocco is generally used for flexible work; calf, being without a grain, is not suitable, as it would show all the creases in the back made by the opening. This class of sewing is excellent for books that do not require so much strength, such as library bindings,[1] but for a dictionary or the like, where constant refe-

[1] This is not to be confounded with public library bindings.

rence or daily use is required, I should sew a book flexibly. Some binders sew their books in the ordinary way, and paste the leather directly to the back, and thus pass it for flexible work; but I do not think any respectable house would do so. *A book that has been sewed flexibly will not have any saw cut in the back,* so that on examination, by opening it wide, it will at once be seen if it is a *real flexible binding or not.*

Intelligence must, however, be used; a book that has already been cased (or bound and sewn on cords) must of necessity have the saw cuts or holes, and such a book would show the cuts.

There is another mode called "*flexible not to show.*" The book is marked up in the usual way as for flexible, and is also slightly scratched on the band marks with the saw; but not deep enough to go through the sections. A thin cord is then taken doubled for each band, and the book is sewn the ordinary flexible way; the cord is knocked into the back in forwarding, and the leather may be stuck on a hollow back with bands, or it may be fastened to the back itself without bands.[1]

However simple it may appear in description to sew a book, it requires great judgment to keep down the swelling of the book to the proper amount necessary to form a good backing groove and no more. In order to do this, the sheets must from time to time be gently tapped down with a piece of wood or a heavy folding-stick, and great care must be observed to avoid drawing the fastening of the kettle stitch too tight, or the head and tail of the book will be thinner than the middle; this fault once committed has no remedy.

If the sections are very thin, or in half sheets, they may, if the book is very thick, be sewn "*two sheets on.*" The needle is passed from the kettle stitch to the first band of

[1] See chapter on Lining up.

the first sheet and out, then another sheet is placed on the top, and the needle inserted at the first band and brought out at band No. 2, the needle is again inserted in the first sheet and in at the second band and out at No. 3, thus treating the two sections as one; in this way it is obvious that only half as much thread will be in the back. With regard to books that have had the heads cut, it will be necessary to open each sheet carefully up to the back before it is placed on the press, otherwise the centre may not be caught, and two or more leaves will be detached after the book is bound.

The first and last sections of every book should be overcast for strength. With regard to books that are composed of single leaves, they are treated of in Chapter III. They are to be overcast, and each section treated as a section of an ordinary book, the only difference being, that a strong lining of paper should be given to the back before covering, so that it cannot "throw up."

When a book is sewn, it is taken from the sewing press by slackening the screws which tighten the beam, so that the cord may be easily detached from the keys and lay cords. The cord may be left at its full length until the end papers are about to be put on, when it must be reduced to about three inches.

Brehmer's patent wire book and pamphlet sewing machine is an introduction well adapted to the use of the stationer, where thick and hand-made paper will bear such a method. It will not, in my opinion, ever be found eligible for library or standard books. Its high price will debar it from the trade generally; but it is to be feared that a sufficient number of really good books may be sewn with it to cause embarrassment to the first-rate binder, who will be baffled in making good work of books which may have been damaged by the invention of sewing books with wire.

The novelty of this machine is, that the book is sewn with wire instead of thread. The machine is fed with wire from spools by small steel rollers, which at each

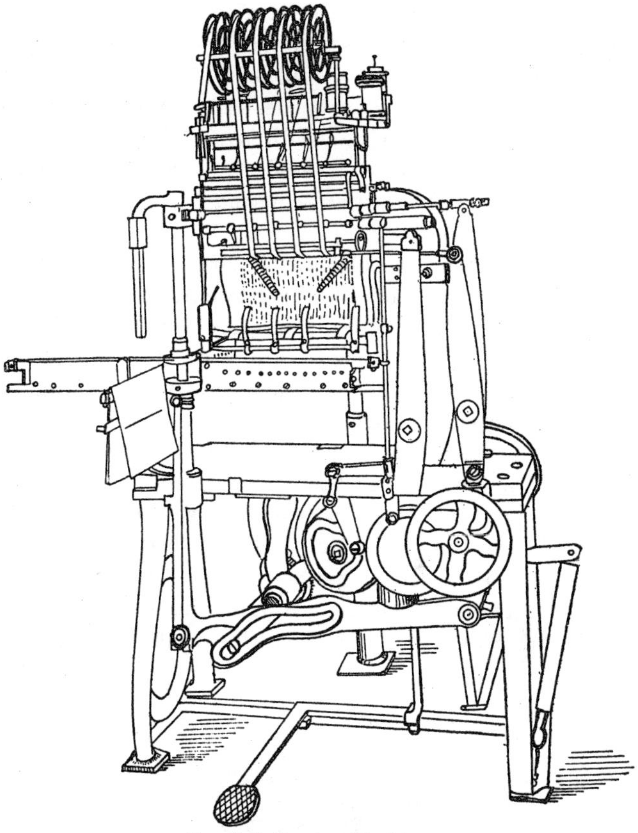

Smythe's Sewing Machine.

revolution supply exactly the length of wire required to form little staples with two legs. Of these staples, the machine makes at every revolution as many as are required for each sheet of the book that is being sewn—generally two or three, or more, as necessary. These wires or staples are forced through the sections from the inside of the folds; and as the tapes are stretched, and held by clasps exactly opposite to each staple-forming and inserting apparatus, the legs of each staple penetrate the tapes, and project through them to a sufficient distance to allow of their being bent inwards towards each other, and pressed firmly against the tapes. With pamphlets, copy-books, catalogues, &c., no tape is used, the staples themselves being sufficient. About two thousand pamphlets or sheets can be sewn in one hour.

Another machine, and I believe the latest, is the "Smythe." The sewer sits in front of the machine and places the sheets, one at a time, on radial arms which project from a vertical rod. These arms rotate, rise, and adjust the sheets, so as to bring them in their proper position under the curved needles. As each arm rises, small holes are pierced, by means of punches in the sheets, from the inside, to facilitate the entrance and egress of the needles. The loopers then receive a lateral movement to tighten the stitch, and this movement is made adjustable, in order that books may be sewn tight or loose, as required. About 20,000 sheets can be sewn in a day, and no previous sawing is required. Thread is used with this machine.

CHAPTER VI.

FORWARDING.

End Papers.—The end papers should always be *made*, that is, the coloured paper pasted to a white one; the style of binding must decide what kind of ends are to be used. I give a slight idea of the kinds of papers used and the method of making them.

Cobb Paper is a paper used generally for half-calf bindings, with a sprinkled edge, or as a change, half-calf, gilt top. The paper is stained various shades and colours in the making, and I think derives its name from a binder who first used it. Being liked by the trade, they have distinguished the paper by calling it "Cobb paper," which name it has kept.

Surface Paper.—This is a paper, one side of which is prepared with a layer of colour, laid on with a brush very evenly. Some kinds are left dull and others are glazed. The darker colours of this paper are generally chosen for Bibles or books of a religious character, and the lighter colours for the cloth or case work. There are many other shades which may be put into extra bindings with very good effect, and will exercise the taste of the workman. For example, a good cream, when of fine colour and good quality, will look very well in a morocco book with either cloth or morocco joints.

Marbled Paper.—This paper has the colour disposed upon it in imitation of marble; hence its name. It is produced by sprinkling properly prepared colours upon the surface of a size, made either of a vegetable emulsion, or of a solution of resinous gum. It is necessary, in either preparing an original design or in matching an example, to remember that the veins are the first splashes of colour thrown on the size, and assume that form in consequence of being driven back by the successive colours employed.

We have it on the authority of Mr. Woolnough,[1] that the old Dutch paper was wrapped round toys in order to evade the duty imposed upon it. After being carefully smoothed out, it was sold to bookbinders at a very high price, who used it upon their extra bindings, and if the paper was not large enough they were compelled to join it. After a time the manufacture was introduced into England, but either the colours are not prepared the same way, or the paper itself may not be so suitable, the colours are not brought out with such vigour and beauty, nor do they stand so well, as on the old Dutch paper. Some secret of the art has been lost, and it baffles our ablest marblers of the present day to reproduce many of the beautiful examples that may be seen in some of the old books.

For further remarks on marbled paper and marbling see chapter on colouring edges.

Printed and other Fancy Paper may be bought at fancy stationers; the variety is so great that description is impossible, but good taste and judgment should always be used by studying the style and colour of binding. Of late years a few firms have paid some attention to this branch, and have placed in the market some very pretty patterns in various tints.

The foreign binders are very fond of papers printed in bronze, and some are certainly of a most elaborate and gorgeous description. Many houses have their own favourite pattern and style. All papers having bronze on

[1] "The Whole Art of Marbling as applied to Paper." C. W. Woolnough. Bell and Sons, 1881.

them should be carefully selected and the cheaper kinds eschewed, the bronze in a short time going black.

Coloured Paste Paper.—This kind the binder can easily make for himself. Some colour should be mixed with paste and a little soap, until it is a little thicker than cream. It should then be spread upon two sheets of paper with a paste brush. The sheets must then be laid together with their coloured surfaces facing each other, and when separated they will have a curious wavy pattern on them. The paper should then be hung up to dry on a string stretched across the room, and when dry glazed with a hot iron. A great deal of it is used in Germany for covering books. Green, reds, and blues have a very good effect.

There are many other kinds of paper that may be used, but the above five different varieties will give a very good idea and serve as points to work from. The many book-binders' material dealers send out pattern books, and in them some hundreds of patterns are to be found.

Before leaving the subject of ends, it may be as well to mention that morocco, calf, russia, silk, etc., are often used on whole bound work; these must, however, be placed in the book when has been covered.

After having decided upon what kind of paper is to be used, two pieces are cut and folded to the size of the book, leaving them a trifle larger, especially if the book has been already cut. Two pieces of white paper must be prepared in the same way. Having them ready, a white paper is laid down, folded, on a pasting board (any old mill-board kept for this purpose), and pasted with moderately thin paste very evenly; the two fancy papers are laid on the top quite even with the back or folded edge; the top fancy paper is now to be pasted, and the other white laid on that: they must now be taken from the board, and after a squeeze in the press between pressing boards, taken out, and hung up separately to dry. This will cause one half of the white to adhere to one half of the marble or fancy paper. When they are dry, they should be refolded in the old folds and pressed for about a quarter of an hour. When there are more than one pair of ends to make, they need not be made one pair at a time, but ten or fifteen pairs may be done at once, by commencing with the one white, then two fancy, two white, and so on, until a sufficient number have been made, always pressing them to ensure the surfaces adhering properly; then hang them up to dry. When dry press again, to make them quite flat. As this is the first time I speak about *pasting*, a few hints or remarks on the proper way will not be out of place here. Always draw the brush well over the paper and away from the centre, towards the edges of the paper. Do not have too much paste in the brush, but just enough to make it slide well. Be careful that the whole surface is pasted; remove all hairs or lumps from the paper, or they will mark the book. Finally, never attempt to take up the brush from the paper before it is well drawn over the edge of the paper, or the paper will stick to the brush and turn over, with the risk of the under side being pasted. While the ends are pressing we will proceed with further forwarding our book.

CHAPTER VII.

Pasting Up.

The first and last sheet of every book must be pasted up or down,—it is called by both terms; and if the book has too much swelling, it must be tapped down gently with a hammer. Hold the book tightly at the foredge with the left hand, knuckles down; rest the back on the press, and hit the back with the hammer to the required thickness. If the book is not held tightly, a portion of the back will slip in and the hollow will always be visible; so I advise that the back be knocked flat on the "lying press" and placed in it without boards, so that the back projects. Screw the press up tightly, so that the sheets cannot slip. A knocking-down iron should then be placed against the book on its left side, and the back hammered against it; the "slips" or cords must be pulled tight, each one being pulled with the right hand, the left holding the slips tightly against the book so that they cannot be pulled through. Should it happen that a slip is pulled out, nothing remains but to re-sew the book, unless it is a thin one, when it may possibly be re-inserted with a large needle. But this will not do the book any good.

The slips being pulled tight, the first and last section should be pasted to those next them. To do this, lay the book on the edge of the press and throw the top section back; lay a piece of waste paper upon the next section about $\frac{1}{8}$ or $\frac{1}{4}$ inch from the back, according to the size of the book, and paste the space between the back and the waste paper, using generally the second finger of the right hand, holding the paper down with the left. When pasted, the waste paper is removed, and the back of the section put evenly with the back of the book, which is now turned over carefully that it may not shift; the other end is treated in the same manner. A weight should then be put on the top, or if more than a single book, one should lie on the top of the other, back and foredge alternately, each book to be half an inch within the foredge of the book next to it, with a few pressing boards on the top one. When dry the end papers are to be pasted on.

CHAPTER VIII.

Putting on the End Papers.

Two single leaves of white paper, somewhat thicker than the paper used for making the ends, are to be cut, one for each side of the book. The end papers are to be laid down on a board, or on a piece of paper on the press to keep them clean, with the pasted or made side uppermost, the single leaves on the top. They should then be fanned out evenly to a proper width, about a quarter of an inch for an 8vo., a piece of waste paper put on the top, and their edges pasted. The slips or cords thrown back, the white fly is put on the book, a little away from the back, and the made ends on the top even with the back, and again left to dry with the weight of a few boards on the top.

If, however, the book or books are very heavy or large, they should have "joints" of either bookbinders' cloth or of leather of the same colour as the leather with which the book is to be covered. Morocco is mostly used for the leather joints. If the joints are to be of cloth, it may be added either when the ends are being put on, or when the book is ready for pasting down. If the cloth joint is to be put on now, the cloth is cut from 1 to 3 inches, according to the size of book, and folded quite evenly, the side of the cloth which has to go on the book being left the width intended to be glued; that is, a width of 1 inch should be folded $\frac{3}{4}$ one side, leaving $\frac{1}{4}$ the other, the latter to be put on the book. The smallest fold is now glued, the white fly put on, and the fancy paper on the top; the difference being, that the paper instead of being made double or folded is single, or instead of taking a paper double the size of the book and folding it, it is cut to the size of the book and pasted all over. It will be better if the marble paper be pasted and the white put on and well rubbed down, and then the whole laid between mill-boards to dry. A piece of waste or brown paper should be slightly fastened at the back over the whole, (turning the cloth down on the book) to keep it clean and prevent it from getting damaged.

The strongest manner is to overcast the ends and cloth joint to the first and last section of the book, as it is then almost impossible either for the cloth or ends to pull away from the book.

If, however, the cloth joint is to be put on after the book is covered, the flys and ends are only edged on with paste to the book just sufficient to hold them while it is being bound; and when the book is to be pasted down, the ends are lifted from the book by placing a thin folding-stick between the ends and book and running it along, when they will come away quite easily. The cloth is then cut and folded as before and fastened on, and the ends and flys properly pasted in the back.

Morocco joints are usually put in after the book is covered, but I prefer that if joints of any kind are to go in the book they should be put in at the same time as the ends. Take great care that the ends are quite dry after being made before attaching them, or the dampness will affect the beginning and end of the book and cause the first few leaves to wrinkle.

When the ends are quite dry the slips should be unravelled and scraped, a bodkin being used for the unravelling, and the back of a knife for the scraping. The object of this is, that they may with greater ease be passed through the holes in the mill-board, and the bulk of the cord be more evenly distributed and beaten down, so as not to be seen after the book has been covered.

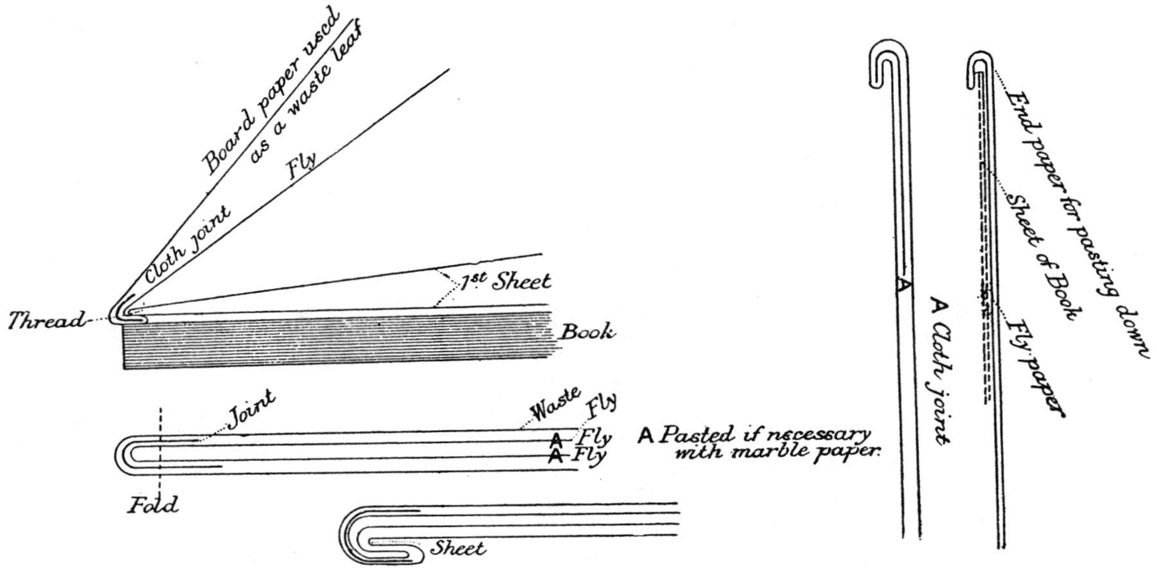

Method of sewing Ends on to Book that cannot tear away.
First and last sheet are not overcasted when treated in this manner.

Many houses cut away the slip entirely, in order that the work may look better. This should never be done; with large and heavy books it is better to allow the bulk of the cord to be seen rather than sacrifice strength. To a certain extent this may be avoided by cutting a small portion of the mill-board away to allow the cord to lodge in.

There is another way of putting on the end papers, that is, to sew the ends on with the book when sewing. The paper is folded at the back with a small fold, the sheet placed in the fold, and the whole sewn through. It is at once apparent that under no circumstances can there be any strain on the ends, and that there is hardly any possibility of the ends breaking away from the sheets.

For books subjected to very hard wear (school books, public library books, etc.) this method of placing the ends is by far the best. See opposite page.

CHAPTER IX.

TRIMMING.

Is the book to have a gilt top? marbled or gilt edges? or is it to be left uncut? These questions must be settled before anything further is done. If the book is to be uncut or have a gilt top, the rough edges should be taken away with a very sharp knife or shears: this process is called "trimming."

The book having been knocked up straight, is laid on a piece of wood planed smooth and kept for this purpose, called a "trimming board." It is then compassed from the back, a straight edge laid to the compass holes, and the foredge cut with a very sharp knife. If the knife is not sharp the paper will yield to the slight pressure required and will not be cut. It is therefore absolutely necessary that a good edge be given to the blade, and, if possible, to keep a special knife for the purpose. Such knives, called trimming knives, are sold, the probable cost being about two shillings. They have a very broad blade.

The object of trimming is to make the edges true; the amount taken off must be only the rough and dirty edges, the book being thus left as large as possible.

The French put their books in the press between boards and rasp the edges, but this method has not only the disadvantage of showing all the marks of the rasp, but also of

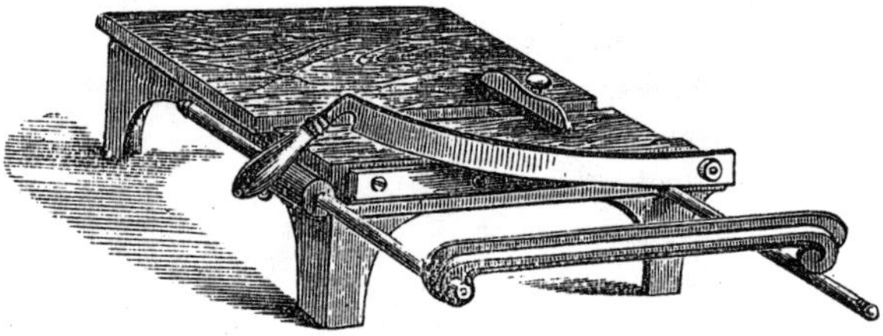

Cardboard Machine used for trimming.

leaving a roughness which catches and retains the dust in proportion to the soft or hard qualities of the paper.

Another method is to put the book into the cutting press, and cut the overplus off with a plough, having a circular knife, called a "round plough." This is used when a number of books are being done together. I prefer to use the straight edge and knife for the foredge and tail, and to cut the top when the book is in boards.

It is, however, not necessary to go to the expense of a round plough, it is only advisable to have one when "plough trimming" is of daily occurrence; an ordinary plough knife, ground to a circular edge, will answer in most cases.

Another excellent plan is to set the gauge of the mill-board machine, or a *card-cutting machine*, and to cut or trim each section, foredge and tail, by the machine knife. In a large number of books this plan is to be recommended; the whole is cut more even and in less time; trimming by this method must, however, be done before sewing. This method is also adopted by some French houses.

Before leaving the subject of trimming, I will insert a few lines from that well-known paper the "Athenæum," as to how a book should be trimmed; and so much do I agree with its writer, that I have the quotation, in large type, hung up in my shop as a constant caution and instruction to the workmen:—

(*No.* 2138, *Oct.* 17*th*, 1868.)

"Mr. Editor,—If you think that the 'Athenæum' is read or seen by any members of that class of ruthless binders, who delight in destroying the appearance of every pamphlet and book that comes into their hands, by trimming or ploughing its edges to the quick (and almost always crookedly), I beg you to insert this appeal to the monsters I have named, to desist from their barbarous practices, to learn to reverence the margin of a book, and never to take from it a hair's breadth more than is absolutely needful. The brutality with which the fair margins of one's loved volumes are treated by these mangling wretches with their awful plough knives is shocking to behold. The curses of book lovers are daily heaped on their backs, but they go on running-a-muck, heedless of remonstrance, remorseless, ever sacrificing fresh victims. Had we a paternal government, one might hope for due punishment of some of these offenders: one at least might be ploughed up the back, another up the front, as an example and a terror to the trade; but as this wholesome correction cannot unhappily be administered, will you give expression to the indignation of one amongst a million sufferers for years from these trimmers' savageries, and let them know what feelings their reckless cruelty awakens in many breasts? One of the largest houses in London has just sent me home fifty copies of an essay, intended as a present for a friend. They have been trimmed, and been ruined. Would that I could have the trimming of their trimmer's hair and ears; also his nose! I don't think his best friend would know him when I had done with him.

"But, Sir, we live in a philanthropic age, and are bound to forgive our enemies and try to reform the worst criminals. I therefore propose a practical measure to win these book trimmers from their enormities; namely, that fifty at least of your readers, who care for book margins, should subscribe a guinea each for a challenge cup, to be competed for yearly, and held by that firm which, on producing copies of all books and pamphlets trimmed by it during the year, shall be adjudged to have disfigured them least. I ask you, Sir, if you will receive subscriptions for this challenge cup? If you will, I shall be glad to send you mine.

"M. A.

"P.S.—Any one who will cut out this letter, and get it pasted up in any binder's or printer's trimming room, will confer a favour on the writer."

A very good trimming machine has been invented by Messrs. Richmond and Co., of Kirby Street, Hatton Garden. The bed rises and falls, with the books upon it, instead of the knife descending upon the work, as in the cutting machines; and the gauges are so arranged, that the foredge of one pile of books, and the tails of another, can be cut at one operation, and it is guaranteed by the makers that the knife will leave a clean and perfectly trimmed edge.

CHAPTER X.

GLUEING UP.

THE book must now be glued up; that is, glue must be applied to the back to hold the sections together, and make the back firm during the rounding and backing. Knock the book perfectly true at its back and head, and put it into the lying press between two pieces of old mill-board; expose the back and let it project from the boards a little, the object being to hold the book firm and to keep the slips close to the sides, so that no glue shall get on them; then with glue, not too thick, but hot, glue the back, rubbing it in with the brush, and take the overplus off again with the brush. In some shops, a handful of shavings is used to rub the glue in, and to take the refuse away, but I consider this to be a bad plan, as a great quantity of glue is wasted.

The Germans rub the glue into the back with the back of a hammer, and take away the overplus with the brush; this is certainly better than using shavings. The back must not be allowed to get too dry before it is rounded, or it will have to be damped with a sponge, to give to the glue the elasticity required, but it should not be wet, this being worse than letting it get too dry. The book should be left for about an hour, or till it no longer feels tacky to the touch, but still retains its flexibility. A flexible bound book should first be rounded, a backing board being used to bring the sheets round instead of a hammer, then the back glued, and a piece of tape tied round the book to prevent its going back flat.

But all books are not glued up in the press; some workmen knock up a number of books, and, allowing them to project a little *over* their press, glue the lot up at once; others again, by holding the book in the left hand and drawing the brush up and down the back. These last methods are, however, only practised in cloth shops, where books are bound or cased at very low prices. The proper way, as I have explained, is to put the book in the lying press. The book is then laid on its side to dry, and if more than one, they should be laid alternately back and foredge, with the back projecting about half an inch, and allowed to dry spontanenusly, and on no account to be dried by the heat of a fire. *All artificial heat in drying in any process of bookbinding is injurious to the work.*

CHAPTER XI.

Rounding.

The word "rounding" applies to the back of the book, and is preliminary to backing. In rounding the back, the book is to be laid on the press before the workman with the foredge towards him; the book is then to be held with the left hand by placing the thumb on the foredge and fingers on the top of the book pointing towards the back, so that by drawing the fingers towards the thumb, or by pressing fingers and thumb together, the back is drawn towards the workman at an angle. In this position the back is struck with the face of the hammer, beginning in the centre, still drawing the back over with the left hand. The book is then to be turned over, and the other side treated in the same way, and continually changed or turned from one side to the other until it has its proper form, which should be a part of a circle. When sufficiently rounded, it should be examined to see if one side be perfectly level with the other, by holding the book up and glancing down its back, and gently tapping the places where uneven, until it is perfectly true or uniform.

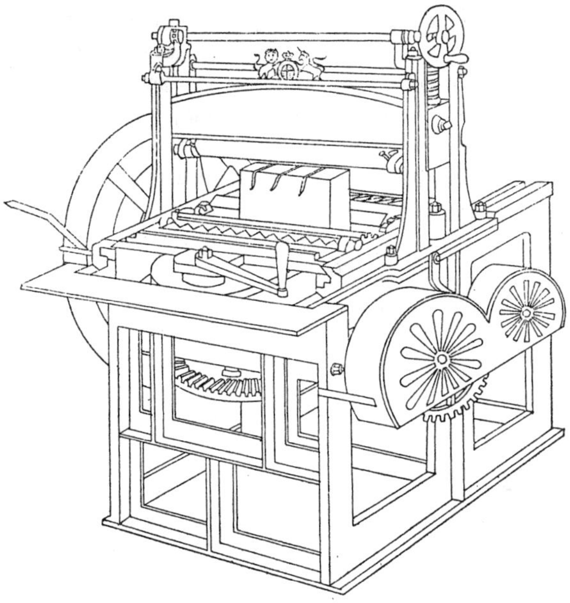

Rounding Machine.

The thicker the book the more difficult it will be found to round it; and some papers will be found more obstinate than others, so that great care must be exercised both in rounding and backing, as the foredge when cut will have exactly the same form as the back. Nothing can be more annoying than to see books lop-sided, pig-backed, and with sundry other ailments, inherent to cheap bookbinding.

The back when properly rounded should be about a third of a circle, according to the present mode, but in olden times they were made almost flat. They were not rounded as now done, but the swelling caused by the thread used made quite enough rounding when put in the press for backing.

Flat back books have a certain charm about them, the more so if in other respects they are properly forwarded. The theory is altogether averse to practical binding. I have always been given to understand that we round our books in order to counteract the tendency of a book to sink in and assume a convex back. Any old well-used book bound with a flat back will show at once this defect.

Messrs. Hopkinson and Cope, of Farringdon Road, London, manufacture a rounding machine. They claim that this machine will round 600 books per hour, and that any desired "round" may be given to the book with great uniformity.

CHAPTER XII.

Backing.

The boards required for backing, called backing boards, should always be the same length as the book. They are made somewhat thicker than cutting boards, and have their tops planed at an angle, so that the sheets may fall well over.

Hold the book in the left hand, lay a board on one side, a little away from the back, taking the edge of the top sheet as a guide, the distance to be a trifle more than the thickness of the boards intended to be used. Then turn over the book, with the backing board, holding the board to the book by the thumb, so that it does not shift, and lay the other board at exactly the same distance on the other side. The whole is now to be held tightly by the left hand and lowered into the press. The boards may possibly have shifted a little during the process, and any correction may now be made whilst the press holds the book before screwing up tight, such as a slight tap with the hammer to one end of a board that may not be quite straight. Should the boards however be not quite true, it will be better to take the whole out and readjust them, rather than

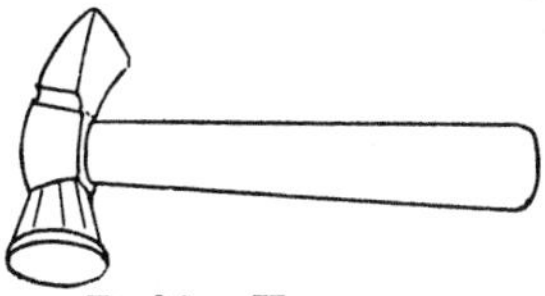

Backing Hammer.

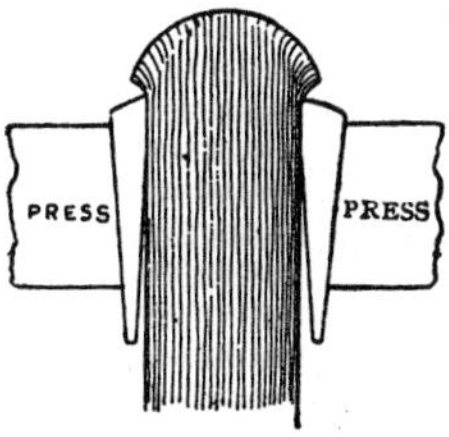

Before Backing.

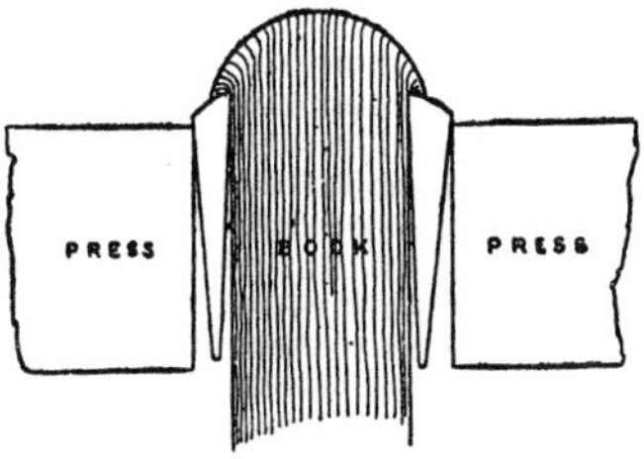

After Backing.

lose time in trying to rectify the irregularity by any other method. If the rounding is not quite true it will be seen at once, and the learner must not be disheartened if he has to take his book out of the press two or three times to correct any slight imperfection.

The book and boards having been lowered flush with the cheeks of the press, screw it up as tightly as possible with the iron hand-pin. The back of the book must now be gently struck with the back of the hammer, holding it slanting and beating the sheets well over towards the backing boards. Commence from the centre of the back and do not hit too hard, or the dent made by the hammer will show after the book has been covered. The back is to be finished with the face of the hammer, the sheets being brought well over on the boards so that a good and solid groove may be made. Each side must be treated in the same way, and have the same amount of weight and beating. The back must have a gradual hammering, and the sheets, when knocked one way, *must not be knocked back again.* The hammer should be swung with a circular motion, always away from the centre of the back. The book, when opened after backing, should be entirely without wrinkles; *their presence being a sign that the workman did not know his business*, or that it was carelessly done. Backing and cutting constitute the chief work in forwarding, and if these two are not done properly the book cannot be square and solid —two great essentials in bookbinding.

Backing flexible work will be found a little more difficult, as the slips are tighter; but otherwise the process is exactly the same, only care must be taken not to hammer the cord too much, and to bring over the sections very gently, in order not to break the sewing thread.

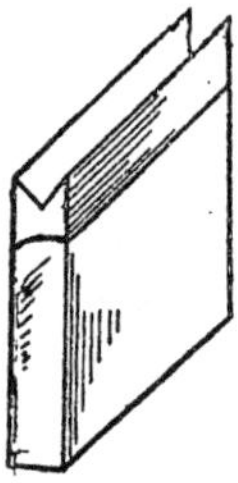

Two-edged Backing Boards.

The backing boards may be replaned from time to time, as they become used, but boards may be had having a double face of steel to them; these may be used from either side. The edges of the steel must not be sharp, or they will cut the paper when backing. The ordinary boards may also have a face of steel screwed to them, but I prefer to use the wood—one can get a firmer back without fear of cutting the sheets.

There are several backing machines by different makers but they are all of similar plan. The book being first rounded is put between the cheeks, and the roller at the top presses the sheets over. I am sorry to say that a great number of sheets get cut by this process, especially when a careless man has charge of the machine.

CHAPTER XIII.

Mill-boards.

There is no occasion to wait for the book to be advanced as far as the backing before the workman sees to his boards; but he should take advantage of the period of drying to prepare them, to look out the proper thickness of the board, and to line them with paper either on one side or on both.

There are now so many kinds of mill-boards made that a few words about them may not be out of place. The best boards are made of old rope, and cost about £30 per ton. The various mills make each a different quality, the prices ranging down to £14 per ton; about this price the straw boards may be said to commence, they going as low as £7, and even less.

A new board has lately appeared called leather board; it is exceedingly hard and durable. I made several experiments with this board, but up to the present have not succeeded in getting it to lay flat on the book.

Boards are made to the various sizes in sheets varying from pott ($17\frac{1}{4} \times 14\frac{1}{4}$ inches) to double elephant (40×28 inches). The thickness is known as *6d.*, *7d.*, *8d.*; 8x, or eightpenny one cross; 8xx, eightpenny two cross; X for tenpenny. Here is a list in full of all the boards likely to be used:—

DESCRIPTION.	SIZE.	6d.		7d.		8d.		8x.		8xx.		X.	
		Dozens in a Bundle.	Weight per Bundle.	Dozens in a Bundle.	Weight per Bundle.	Dozens in a Bundle.	Weight per Bundle.	Dozens in a Bundle.	Weight per Bundle.	Dozens in a Bundle.	Weight per Bundle.	Dozens in a Bundle.	Weight per Bundle.
	inches.		lb.		lb.		lb.		lb.		lb.		lb.
Pott	$17\frac{1}{4} \times 14\frac{1}{4}$	6	28	6	40	5	48	5	56	4	60	3	58
Foolscap	$18\frac{1}{2} \times 14\frac{1}{2}$	6	32	6	44	5	50	5	58	4	62	3	58
Crown	$20 \times 16\frac{1}{4}$	6	36	6	50	5	62	5	72	4	74	3	72
Small Half Royal.	$20\frac{1}{4} \times 13$	6	30	6	44	5	50	5	60	4	62	3	58
Large Half Royal.	21×14	6	30	6	48	5	60	5	62	4	70	3	72
Short	21×17	6	38	6	55	5	70	5	78	4	78	3	78
Sm. Half Imperial	$22\frac{1}{4} \times 15$	6	36	6	50	5	64	4	70	3	62	2	60
Half Imperial ..	$23\frac{1}{2} \times 16\frac{1}{2}$	6	40	6	60	5	66	4	70	3	66	2	64
Mdle. or Sm. Demy	$22\frac{1}{2} \times 18\frac{1}{2}$	6	45	6	60	5	66	4	74	3	72	2	66
Large Middle or Large Demy	$23\frac{3}{4} \times 18\frac{1}{2}$	6	48	6	68	5	66	4	76	3	74	2	60
Large or Medium	24×19	6	48	6	70	5	65	4	76	3	74	2	60
Small Royal ..	$25\frac{1}{2} \times 19\frac{1}{2}$	6	52	6	78	5	78	4	84	3	84	2	68
Large Royal ..	$26\frac{3}{4} \times 20\frac{3}{4}$	6	52	6	78	4	68	3	76	2	68	2	86
Extra Royal ..	$28\frac{1}{2} \times 21\frac{1}{2}$	6	56	6	82	4	74	3	80	2	74	2	92
Imperial	$32 \times 22\frac{1}{2}$	6	72	4	72	3	72	2	72	2	96	2	120

Having chosen the board, it is necessary to cut it up to the size wanted. If the book is 8vo., the board is cut into eight pieces; if 4to., into four; using a demy board for a demy book, or a royal for a royal book. To cut up the board, first mark up, as a guide for the mill-board

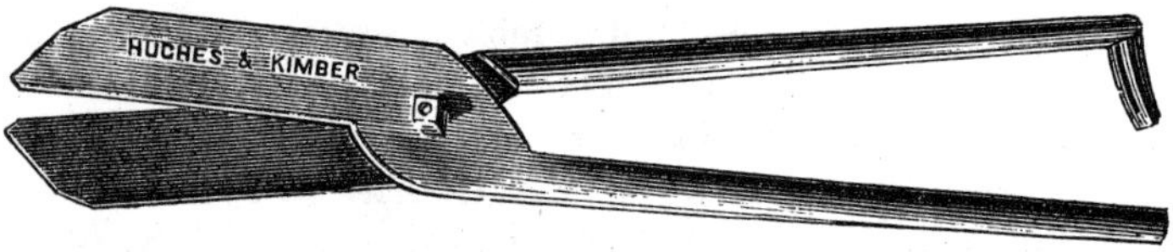

Mill-board Shears.

shears. These are very large shears, in shape somewhat like an enlarged tin shears. To use the shears, screw up one arm in the laying press, hold the board by the left hand, using the right to work the upper arm, the left hand meanwhile guiding the board. Some little tact is required to cut heavy boards. It will be found that it is necessary to press the lower arm away with the thigh, and bring the upper arm towards the operator whilst cutting.

A mill-board cutting machine is now in all large shops. The cut fairly well explains itself; the long blade descending cuts the boards, which are held fast on the table by the clamp. The gauges are set either on the table or in front. The board is put on the table and held tight by pressure of

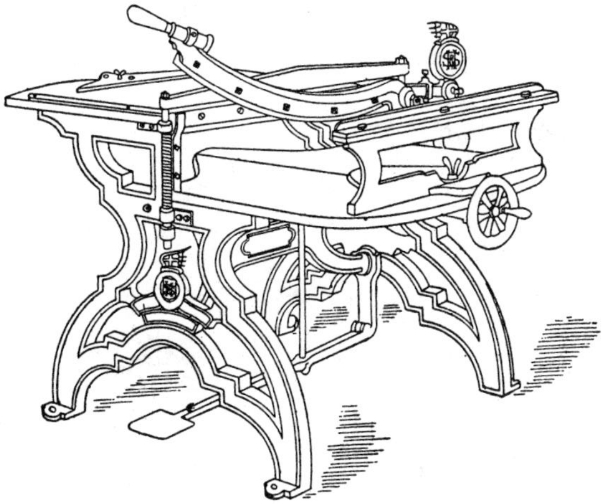

Mill-board Machine.

the foot on the treadle; the knife descending upon the exposed board cuts after the principle of the guillotine blade. Another kind, introduced by Messrs. Richmond, of Kirby Street, Hatton Garden, is made for steam work, and is no doubt one of the best that can be made. Instead of a knife to descend, a number of circular cutters are made to revolve on two spindles, the one cutter working against the other (see woodcut); but I give Messrs. Richmond's own description, it being more explicit than any I could possibly give: "The machine accomplishes a surprising amount of superior work in a very short time, and the best description of the ordinary lever mill-board cutting machine cannot be compared with it. The machine is very strongly and accurately constructed. It is furnished with an iron table having a planed surface, and is also provided with a self-acting feed gauge. The gear wheels are engine cut, and the circular cutters, which are of the

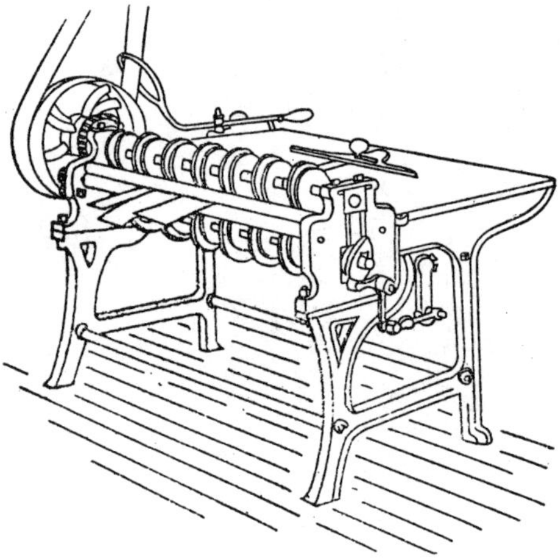

Steam Mill-board Cutting Machine.

best cast steel, being turned and ground "dead true," clean and accurate cutting is insured. The machine will therefore be found to be a most profitable acquisition to any bookbinding establishment in which large quantities of mill-board are used up."

The boards being cut, square the edge which is to go to the back of the book. This must be done in the cutting press, using a cutting board for one side termed a "runner," and another called a "cut-against" for the other side.

These are simply to save the press from being cut; and a piece of old mill-board is generally placed on the cut-against, so that the plough knife does not cut or use up the cut-against too quickly. The boards are now, if for whole-binding, to be lined on both sides with paper; if for half-binding only on one side. The reason for lining them is to make the boards curve inwards towards the book. The various pastings would cause the board to curve the contrary way if it were not lined. If the boards are to be lined both sides, paper should be cut double the size of the boards; if only one side, the paper cut a little wider than the boards, so that a portion of the paper may be turned over on to the other side about a quarter of an inch. The paper is now pasted with not too thick paste, and the board laid on the paper *with the cut edge towards* the portion to be turned over. It is now taken up with the paper adhering, and laid down on the press with the paper side upwards, and rubbed well down; it is then again turned over and the paper drawn over the other side. It is advisable to press the boards to make more certain of the paper adhering, remembering always that the paper must be pasted all over very evenly, for it cannot be expected to adhere if it is not pasted properly.

When the books are very thick, two boards must be pasted together, not only to get the proper thickness, but for strength, for a made board is always stronger than a single one. If a board has to be made, a thick and a somewhat thinner board should be fastened together *with paste.* Paste both boards and put them in the standing press for the night. Great pressure should not be put on at first, but after allowing them to set for a few minutes, pull down the press as tight as possible. When placing made boards to the book, *the thinner one should always be next the book.* It may be taken as a general rule that a thinner board when pasted will always draw a thicker one.

When boards are lined on one side only it is usual to turn half an inch of the paper over the square or cut edge, and the lined side must be placed next the book.

Many binders line the mill-board all over with paper before cutting; this may save time, but the edge of the board at the joint is liable to be abraised, and the resulting joint uneven.

The boards when lined should be laid about or stood up to dry, and when dry, cut to the proper and exact size for the book. As a fact, the black boards now sold are much too new or green to be used direct by the binder, they should be stocked for some months.

The requisite width is obtained by extending the compass from the back of the book to the edge of the smallest bolt or fold in the foredge. It is advisable not to measure less than this point, but to leave a leaf or two in order to show that the book is not cut down. The compasses being fixed by means of the side screw, the boards are to be knocked up even, compassed up, and placed in the lying press, in which they are cut, using, as before, the "cut-against," and placing the runner exactly to the compass holes. When cut they are to be tested by turning one round and putting them together again; if they are the least out of truth it will be apparent at once. The head or top of the boards is next to be cut by placing a square against the back and marking the head or top with a bodkin or point of a knife. The boards being quite straight are again put into the press and cut, and when taken out should be again proved by reversing them as before, and if not true they must be recut. The length is now taken from the head of the book to the tail, and in this some judgment must be used. If the book has already been cut the measure must be somewhat larger than the book, allowing only such an amount of paper to be cut off as will make the edge smooth. If, however, the book is to be entirely uncut, the size of the book is measured, and in addition the portion called *squares* must be added.

When a book has not been cut, the amount that is to be cut off the head will give the head or top square, and the book being measured from the head, another square or projection must be added to it, and the compass set to one of the shortest leaves in the book. Bearing in mind the article on trimming, enough of the book *only* should be cut to give the edge solidity for either gilding or marbling. A few leaves should always be left not cut with the plough, to show that the book has not been cut down. These few leaves are called *proof*, and are always a mark of careful work.

About twenty years ago it was the mode to square the foredge of the boards, then lace or draw them in, and to cut the head and tail of the boards and book together, then to turn up and cut the foredge of the book.

CHAPTER XIV.

Drawing-in and Pressing.

The boards having been squared, they are to be attached to the book by lacing the ends of the cord through holes made in the board. The boards are to be laid on the book with their backs in the groove and level with the head; they must then be marked either with a lead pencil or the point of a bodkin exactly in a line with the slips, about half an inch down the board. On a piece of wood the millboard is placed, and holes are pierced by hammering a short bodkin through on the line made, at a distance from the edge in accordance with the size of the book. About half an inch away from the back is the right distance for an octavo. The board is then to be turned over, and a second hole made about half an inch away from the first ones. The boards having been holed, the slips must be scraped, pasted slightly, and tapered or pointed. Draw them tightly through the hole first made and back through the second. Tap them slightly when the board is down to prevent them from slipping and getting loose. When the cords are drawn through, cut the ends close to the board with a knife, and well hammer them down on the knocking-down iron to make the board close on the slips and hold them tight. The slips should be well and carefully hammered, as any projection will be seen with great distinctness when the book is covered. The hammer must be held perfectly even, for the *slips will be cut* by the edge of it if *used carelessly*.

The book is now to be examined, and any little alteration may be made before putting it into the standing press. With all books, a tin should be placed between the millboard and book, to flatten the slips, and prevent their adherence. The tin is placed right up to the groove, and serves also as a guide for the pressing board. Pressing boards, the same size as the book, should be put flush with the groove, using the pressing tin as guide, and the book or books placed in the centre of the press directly under the screw, which is to be tightened as much as possible. In pressing books of various sizes, the largest book must always be put at the bottom of the press, with a block or a few pressing boards between the various sizes, in order to get equal pressure on the whole, and to allow the screw to come exactly on the centre of the books.

The backs of the books are now to be pasted, and allowed to stand for a few minutes to soften the glue. Then with a piece of wood or iron, called a cleaning-off stick (wood is preferable), the glue is rubbed off, and the backs are well rubbed with a handful of shavings and left to dry. Leave them as long as possible in the press, and if the volume is rather a thick one a coat of paste or thin glue should be applied to the back. Paste is preferable.

If the book is very thick a piece of thin calico may be pasted to the back and allowed to dry, the surplus being taken away afterwards.

In flexible work care must be taken that the cleaning-off stick is not forced too hard against the bands, or the thread being moist will break, or the paper being wet will tear, or the bands may become shifted. The cleaning-off stick may be made of any piece of wood; an old octavo cutting board is as good as anything else, but a good workman will always have one suitable and at hand when required for use.

When the volumes have been pressed enough (a day's pressing is none too much) they are to be taken out, and the tins and pressing boards put away. The book is then ready for cutting. Of the numerous presses, excepting the hydraulic, Gregory's Patent Compound Action Screw Press is to my mind the best, and I believe it to be one of the most powerful presses yet invented; sixty tons pressure can be obtained by it.

CHAPTER XV.

Cutting.

In olden times, when our present work-tools did not exist and material aids were scarce, a sharp knife and straight edge formed the only implements used in cutting. Now we have the plough and cutting machine, which have superseded the knife and straight edge; and the cutting machine is now fast doing away with the plough. There are very few shops at the present moment where a cutting machine is not in use, in fact I may say that, without speaking only of cloth books, for they must always be cut by machinery owing to the price not allowing them to be done otherwise, there are very few books, not even excepting extra books, that have escaped the cutting machine.

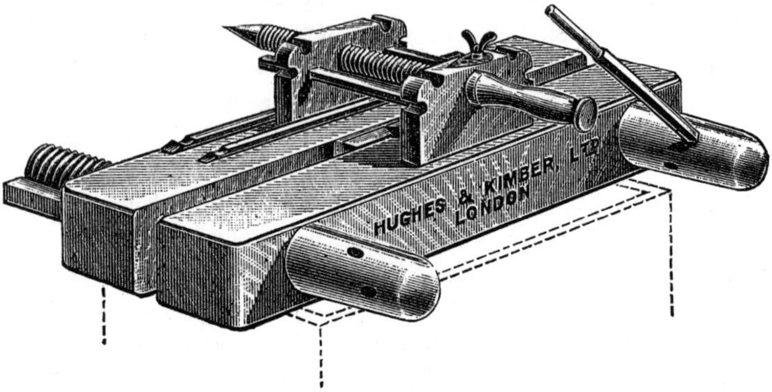

Cutting Press and Plough.

All cutting "presses" are used in the same way. The plough running over the press, its left cheek running between two guides fastened on the left cheek of the press. By turning the screw of the plough the right cheek is advanced towards the left; the knife fixed on the right of

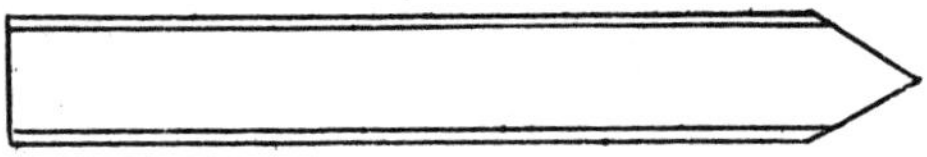

Sliding Knife.

the plough is advanced, and with the point cuts gradually through the boards or paper secured in the press, as already described in preparing the boards. There are two kinds of ploughs in use—in one the knife is bolted, in the other the knife slides in a dovetail groove—termed respectively "bolt knife" and "slide knife." The forwarder will find that the latter is preferable, on account of its facility of action, as any length of knife can be exposed for cutting. But with a bolt knife, being fastened to the shoe of the plough, it is necessarily a fixture, and must be worn down by cutting or squaring mill-boards, or such work, before it can be used with the truth necessary for paper.

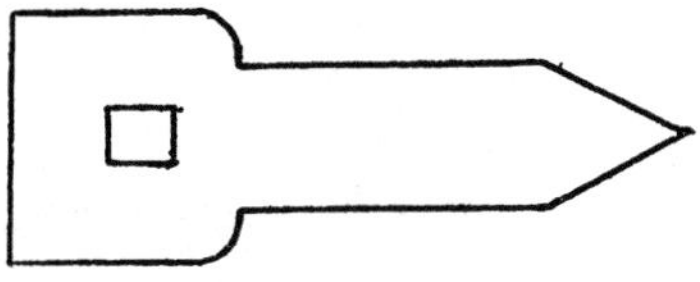

Bolt Knife.

To cut a book properly it must be quite straight, and the knife must be sharp and perfectly true. Having this in mind, the book may be cut by placing the front board the requisite distance from the head that is to be cut off. A piece of thin mill-board or trindle is put between the hind board and book, so that the knife when through the book may not cut the board. The book is now to be lowered into the cutting press, with the back towards the workman, until the front board is exactly on a level with the press. The head of the book is now horizontal with the press, and the amount to be cut off exposed above it. Both sides should be looked to, as the book is very liable to get a twist in being put in the press. When it is quite square the press is to be screwed up tightly and evenly. Each end should be screwed up to exactly the same tightness, for if one end is loose the paper will be jagged or torn instead of being cut cleanly.

The book is cut by drawing the plough gently to and fro; each time it is brought towards the workman a slight amount of turn is given to the screw of the plough. If too much turn is given to the screw, the knife will bite too deeply into the paper and *will tear instead of cutting it.* If the knife has not been properly sharpened, or has a burr upon its edge, it will be certain to cause ridges on the paper. The top edge being cut, the book is taken out of the press and the *tail* cut. A mark is made on the top of the hind or back board just double the size of the square, and the board is lowered until the mark is on a level with the cut top. The book is again put into the press, with the back towards the workman, until the board is flush with the cheek of the press; this will expose above the press the amount to be taken off from the tail, as before described, and the left hand board will be, if put level with the cut top, exactly the same distance above the press as the right hand board is below the cut top. The tail is cut in the same way as the top edge.

To cut a book properly requires great care. It will be of great importance to acquire a methodical exactness in working the different branches, cutting especially. Always lay a book down one way and take it up another, and in cutting always work with the back of the book towards you, and cut from you. Give the turn to the screw of the plough as it is thrust from you, or you will pull away a part of the back instead of cutting it.

In cutting the foredge, to which we must now come, always have the head of the book towards you, so that if not cut straight you know exactly where the fault lies. The foredge is marked both back and front of the book by placing a cutting board under the first two or three leaves as a support; the mill-board is then pressed firmly into the groove and a line is drawn or a hole is pierced head and tail, the foredge of the board being used as a guide. The book is now knocked with its back on the press quite flat, and trindles (flat pieces of steel in the shape of an elongated U, about 1½ inch wide and 3 or 4 inches long, with a slot nearly the whole length) are placed between the boards and book by letting the boards fall back from the book and then passing one trindle at the head, the other at tail, allowing the top and bottom slip to go in the grooves of the trindles. The object of this is to force the back up quite flat, and by holding the book when the cut-against and runner is on it, supported by the other hand under the boards, it can be at once seen if the book is straight or not. The cut-against must be put quite flush with the holes on

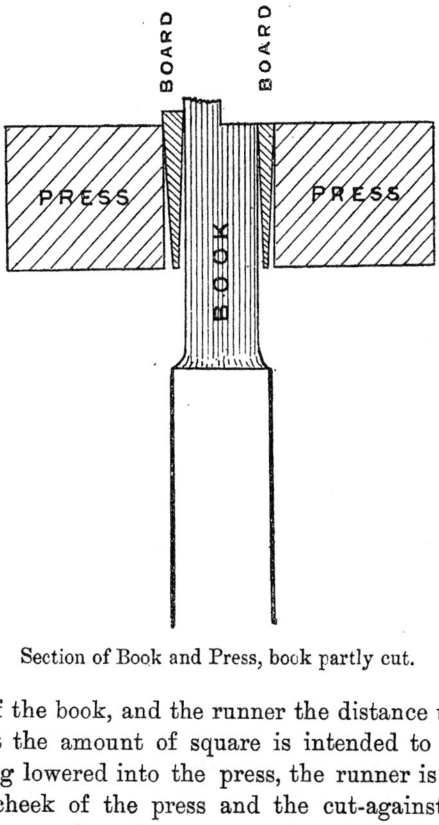

Section of Book and Press, book partly cut.

the left of the book, and the runner the distance under the holes that the amount of square is intended to be. The book being lowered into the press, the runner is put flush with the cheek of the press and the cut-against just the same distance *above* the press as the runner is *below* the holes. The trindles must be taken out from the book when the cutting boards are in their proper place, and the mill-boards will then fall down. The book and cutting boards must be held very tightly or they will slip and, if the book has been lowered into the press accurately, everything will be quite square. The press must now be screwed up tightly, and the foredge ploughed; when the book is taken out of the press it will resume its original rounding, the foredge will have the same curve as the back, and if cut truly there will be a proper square all round the edges. This method is known as "cutting in boards."

If the amateur or workman has a set of some good work which he wishes to bind uniformly, but which has already been cut to different sizes, and he does not wish to cut the large ones down to the smaller size, he must not draw the small ones in, as he may possibly not be able to pull the boards down the required depth to cut the book, but he must leave the boards loose, cut the head and tail, then draw the boards in, and turn up and cut the foredge.

"Cutting out of boards" is by a different method. The foredge is cut before gluing up, if for casing, taking the size *from the case*, from the back to the edge of the board in the foredge. The book is then glued up, rounded, and put into the press for half an hour, just to set it. The size is again taken from the case, allowing for squares head and tail. The book having been marked is cut, and then backed. Cloth cases are made for most periodicals, and may be procured from their publishers at a trifling cost, which varies according to the size of the book and the amount of blocking that is upon them.

This method of cutting out of boards is adopted in many of the cheap shops (even leather shops). It is a method, however, not to be commended.

To test if the book be cut true it is only necessary to turn the top leaf back level to the back of the book and even at the head; if it be the slightest bit untrue it will at once be seen.

A few words about the various cutting machines that are in the market. Each maker professes his machine the

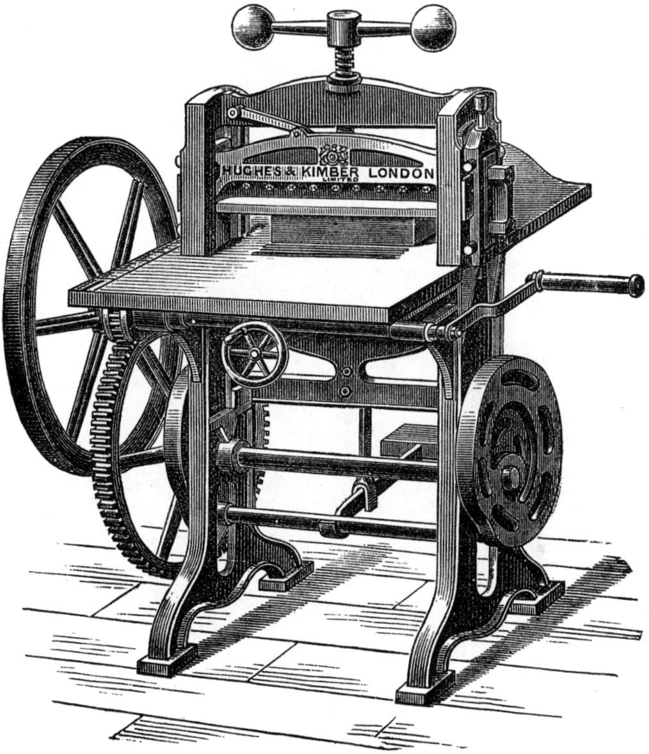

Cutting Machine.

best. In some the knife moves with a diagonal motion, in others with a horizontal motion.

The principle of all these machines is the same: the books are placed to a gauge, the top is lowered and clamps the book, and, on the machine being started, the knife descends and cuts through the paper.

Another machine by Harrild and Son, called a registered cutting machine, is here illustrated. Its operation is on the same principle as a lying press, the difference being, that this has a table upon which the work is placed; a

Registered Cutting Machine.

gauge is placed at the back so that the work may be placed against it for accuracy, the top beam is then screwed down and the paper ploughed. A great amount of work may be accomplished with this machine, and to anyone that cannot afford an ordinary cutting machine this will be found invaluable.

CHAPTER XVI.

Colouring the Edges.

The edges of every book must be in keeping with the binding. A half roan book should not have an expensive edge, neither a whole bound morocco book a sprinkled edge. Still, no rule has been laid down in this particular, and taste should regulate this as it must in other branches. The taste of the public is so changeable that it is impossible to lay down any rule, and I leave my reader to his own discretion.

Here are various ways in which the edges may be coloured.

Sprinkled Edges.—Most shops have a colour always ready, usually a reddish brown, which they use for the whole of their sprinkled edge books. The colour can be purchased at any oil shop. A mixture of burnt umber and red ochre is generally used. The two powders must be well mixed together in a mortar with paste, a few drops of sweet oil, and water. The colour may be tested by sprinkling some on a piece of white paper, allowing it to dry, and then burnishing it. If the colour powders or rubs, it is either too thick, or has not enough paste in it. If the former, some water must be added; if the latter, more paste: and it will perhaps be better if the whole is passed through a cloth to rid it of any coarse particles. The books may be sprinkled so as to resemble a kind of marble by using two or three different colours. For instance, the book is put in the lying press and a little sand is strewn upon the edge in small mounds. Then with a green colour a moderate sprinkle is given. After allowing it to dry, more sand is put on in various places, a dark sprinkle of brown is put on, and the whole allowed to dry. When the sand is shaken off, the edge will be white where the first sand was dropped, green where the second, and the rest brown.

A colour of two shades may be made by using sand, then a moderately dark brown sprinkled, then more sand, and lastly a deeper shade of same colour.

There are a few of the "*Old Binders*" who still use what is called the "finger brush," a small brush about the size of a shaving brush, made of stiff bristles cut squarely. They dip it into the colour, and then by drawing the finger across it jerk the colour over the edge. Another method is to use

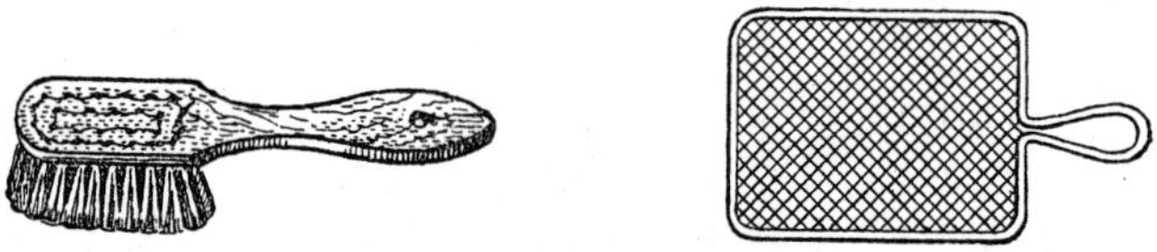

Sprinkling Brush and Sieve.

a larger brush, which being dipped in the colour is beaten on a stick or press-pin until the desired amount of sprinkle is obtained. But the best plan is to use a nail brush and a common wire cinder sifter. Dip the brush in the colour and rub it in a circular direction over the cinder sifter. This mode has the satisfactory result of doing the work quicker, finer, and more uniformly. The head, foredge and tail must be of exactly the same shade, and one end must not have more sprinkle on it than the other, and a set of books should have their edges precisely alike in tone and colour.

Colours for Sprinkling.—To give an account of how the various colours are made that were formerly used would be only waste of time, as so many dyes and colours that answer all purposes may be purchased ready for instant use. I may with safety recommend Judson's dyes diluted with water.

Plain Colouring.—The colour having been well ground is to be mixed with paste and a little oil, or what is perhaps better, glaire and oil. Then with a sponge or with a brush colour the whole of the edge. In colouring the foredge the book should be drawn back so as to form a slope of the edge, so that when the book is opened a certain amount of colour will still be seen. It is often necessary to give the edges two coats of colour, but the first must be quite dry before the second is applied.

A very good effect may be produced by first colouring the edge yellow, and when dry, after throwing on rice, seeds, pieces of thread, fern leaves, or anything else according to fancy, then sprinkling with some other dark colour. For this class of work body sprinkling colour should always be used. It may be varied in many different ways.

Marbled Edges.—The edges of marbled books should in almost every instance correspond with their marbled ends.

In London very few binders marble their own work, but send it out of the house to the *Marblers*, who do nothing else but make marbled edges and paper. One cannot do better than send one's books to be marbled; it will cost only a few pence, which will be well spent in avoiding the trouble and dirt that marbling occasions; nevertheless I will endeavour to explain; it is, however, a process that may seem very easy, but is very difficult to execute properly.

The requisites are a long square wooden or zinc trough about 2 inches deep to hold the size for the colours to float on; the dimensions to be regulated by the work to be done. About 16 to 20 inches long and 6 to 8 inches wide will probably be large enough. Various colours are used, such as lake, rose, vermilion, king's yellow, yellow ochre,

Prussian blue, indigo, some green, flake white, and lamp black. The brushes for the various colours should be of moderate size, and each pot of colour must have its own brush. Small stone jars are convenient for the colours, and a slab of marble and muller to grind them must be provided. The combs may be made with pieces of brass wire about two inches long, inserted into a piece of wood; several of these will be required with the teeth at different distances, according to the width of the pattern required to be produced. Several different sized burnishers, flat and round, will be required for giving a gloss to the work.

The first process in marbling is the preparation of the size on which the colours are to be floated. This is a solution of *gum tragacanth*, or as it is commonly called, gum

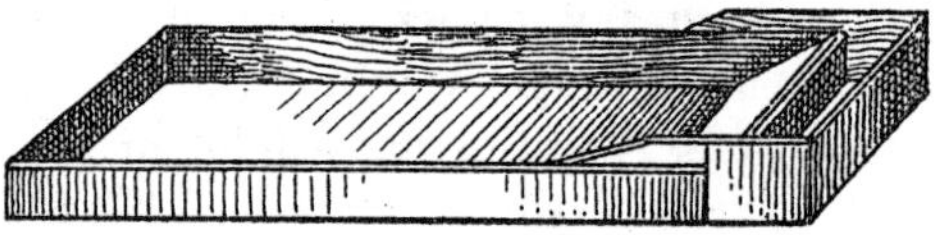

Marbling Trough.

dragon. If the gum is placed over night in the quantity of water necessary it will generally be found dissolved by the morning. The quantity of gum necessary to give proper consistency to the size is simply to be learned by experience, and cannot be described; and the solution must always be filtered through muslin or a linen cloth before use.

The colours must be ground on the marble slab with a little water, as fine as possible; move the colour from time to time into the centre of the marble with a palette knife, and as the water evaporates add a little more. About one oz. of colour will suffice to grind at once, and it will take about two hours to do it properly.

Having everything at hand and ready, with the size in

the trough, and water near, the top of the size is to be carefully taken off with a piece of wood the exact width of the trough, and the colour being well mixed with water and a few drops of *ox gall*, a little is taken in the brush, and a *few very fine* spots are thrown on.

If the colour does not spread out, but rather sinks down, a few more drops of gall must be carefully added and well mixed up. The top of the size must be taken off as before described, and the colour again thrown on.

If it does not then spread out, the ground or size is of too thick consistency, and some clean water must be added, and the whole well mixed.

If the colour again thrown on spreads out, but looks rather greyish or spotty, then the colour is too thick, and a little water must be added, but very carefully, lest it be made too thin. If the colour still assumes a greyish appearance when thrown on, then the fault lies in the grinding, and it must be dried and again ground.

When the colour, on being thrown on, spreads out in very large spots, the ground or size is too thin and a little thicker size should be added. Now, if the consistency or the amount of gum water be noticed, by always using the same quantity the marbler cannot fail to be right.

If the colours appear all right on the trough, and when taken off on a slip of paper adhere to it, the size and colours are in perfect working order.

The top of the size must always be taken off with the piece of wood before commencing work, so that it be kept clean, and the colours must always be well shaken out of the brush into the pot before sprinkling, so that the spots may not be too large. The marbler must always be guided by the pattern he wishes to produce, and by a little thought he will get over many difficulties that appear of greater magnitude than they really are.

Spot Marble.—The size is first to be sprinkled with a

dark colour, and this is always termed the "ground colour," then the other colours; bearing in mind that the colour that has the most gall will spread or push the others away, and this colour should in spot marbling be put on last.

With very little variation all the other kinds of marbling are done; but in every case where there are more books or sheets of paper to be done of the same pattern than the trough will take at once, the same order of colours must be kept, and the same proportion of each, or one book will be of one colour and the second entirely different.

Comb or Nonpareil Marble.—The colours are to be thrown on as before, but as fine as possible. Then if a piece of wood or wire be drawn backwards and forwards across the trough, the colours, through the disturbance of the size, will follow the motion of the stick. A comb is then to be drawn the whole length of the trough in a contrary direction. The wire in the comb will draw the colour, and thus will be produced what is termed comb or nonpareil marble.

The size or width of the teeth of the comb will vary the size of the marble.

Spanish Marble.—The ground colour is to be thrown on rather heavily, the others lighter, and the wavy appearance is caused by gently drawing the paper in jerks over the marble, thus causing the colour to form small ripples.

A few drops of turpentine put in the colours will give them a different effect, viz.,—causing the small white spots that appear on the *shell marble.*

There are various patterns, each being known by name: old Dutch, nonpareil, antique, curl, Spanish, shell. An apprentice would do well to go to some respectable shop and ask for a sheet or two of the various kinds mentioned, and as each pattern is given to him, write the name on the back, and always keep it as a pattern for future use and reference.

Edges are marbled, after making the desired pattern on the trough by holding the book firmly, pressing the edge on the colour and lifting it up sharply. The foredge must be made flat by knocking the book on its back, but the marbler had better tie his book between a pair of backing boards, so that it may not slip, especially with large books. Care must be taken with books that have many plates, or if the paper is at all of a spongy nature or unsized. If a little cold water be thrown on the edges it will cause the colours to set better. In marbling writing paper, a sponge with a little alum water should be used to take off the gloss or shine from the edge, occasioned by the cutting knife, and to assist the marbling colour to take better.

Paper is marbled in the same way by holding it at two corners; then gently putting it on the colour and pressing it evenly, but gently all over, so that the colour may take on every part. It must be lifted carefully, as the least shake by disturbing the size will spoil the regularity of the pattern. Paper should be damped over night and left with a weight on the top. When the paper has been marbled and is dry, a rag with a little bee's wax or soap should be rubbed over it, so that the burnisher may not stick, and may give a finer gloss; this applies also to the edges in burnishing. Marble paper manufacturers burnish the paper with a piece of polished flint or glass fixed in a long pole working in a socket at the top, the other end resting on a table which is slightly hollowed, so that the segment of the circle which the flint takes is exactly that of the hollow table. The paper is laid on the hollow table, and the burnisher is worked backwards and forwards until the desired gloss is attained. By the best and latest method, the paper is passed between highly polished cylinders. It is more expensive, on account of the cost of the machinery, but insures superior effect.

A great deal of paper is now being made by means of a

mechanical process. It has a very high gloss; it is used on very cheap work.

Sizing.—Paper should be always sized after being marbled. The size is made by dissolving one pound of best glue in five gallons of water with half a pound of best white soap. This is put into a copper over night, and on a low fire the next morning, keeping it constantly stirred to prevent burning. When quite dissolved and hot it is passed through a cloth into a trough, and each sheet passed through the liquor and hung up to dry; when dry, burnish as above.

But it will be far cheaper to buy the paper, rather than make it at the cost of more time than will be profitable. The charge for demy size is at the rate of 20*s.* to 95*s.* per ream, according to the quality and colour; but to those to whom money is no object, and who would prefer to make their own marbled paper, I hope the foregoing explanation will be explicit enough.

The "English Mechanic," March 17th, 1871, has the following method of transferring the pattern from ordinary marble paper to the edges of books:—

"Ring the book up tightly in the press, the edge to be as flat as possible; cut strips of the best marble paper about one inch longer than the edge, make a pad of old paper larger than the edge of the book, and about a quarter inch thick; then get a piece of blotting paper and a sponge with a little water in; now pour on a plate sufficient spirits of salts (muriatic acid) to saturate the paper, which must be placed marble side downwards on the spirit (not dipped in it); when soaked put it on the edge (which has been previously damped with a sponge), lay your blot paper on it, then your pad, now rap it smartly all over, take off the pad and blot, and look if the work is right, if so, take the book out and shake the marble paper off; when dry burnish."

At a lecture delivered at the Society of Arts, January,

1878, by Mr. Woolnough, a practical marbler, the whole process of marbling was explained. Mr. Woolnough has since published an enlarged treatise on marbling,[1] and one that should command the attention of the trade. A copy of the Society's journal can be had, describing the process, No. 1,314, vol. XXVI., and will be of great service to any reader, but his work is more exhaustive.

Leo's Mechanical Marblers.

A transfer marble paper may now be had, and from examples sent me the process seems fairly workable. The following is the method of working sent by the importers of the paper:—

"Place the book in the press. The book edge which is to be marbled has to be rubbed with pure spirits of wine; the dry strip of transfer marble is then to be put on the edge. The white back or reverse side, whilst being pressed hard against the book edge, is to be moistened carefully with boiling water, by dabbing a saturated sponge on it; this dabbing process to be continued so long till the colour will show through the white back —a proof that it is loosened from the paper. Then remove the white paper, and let the edge dry slowly. When quite dry burnish."

Leo's Mechanical Marblers.

Another invention is to marble the edges by means of one or more rollers. The top roller or rollers holds the colour, which is distributed on the under rollers; these, in turn, ink the edge on being passed over it. The books are naturally held in the press whilst this is being done.

[1] George Bell and Sons, York Street, Covent Garden.

From a book, the "School of Arts," third edition, 1750, which has a chapter on marbling, the following, with cut, is taken :—

"When thus you have your colours and all things in good order, then take a pencil, or the end of a feather, and sprinkle or put first your red colour; then the blue,

Cut from Book "School of Arts," 1750.

yellow, green, etc. Begin your red from No. 1, and go along your trough to No. 2, also the blue from No. 3, all along to No. 4; the yellow and green put here and there in the vacant plaees. Then with a bodkin or a small skewer draw a sort of a serpentine figure through the colours, beginning from No. 1 to No. 2; when this is done, then take your comb and draw the same straight along from

No. 1 to No. 2. If you have some turnings or snail work on your paper, then with a bodkin give the colours what turns you please. (See the plate.)

"Thus far you are ready in order to lay on your paper, which must be moistened the day before, in the same manner as book-printers do their paper for printing; take a sheet at a time, lay it gently upon your colours in the trough, press it slightly with your finger down in such places where you find the paper lies hollow; this done, take hold at one end of the paper, and draw it up at the other end of the trough;

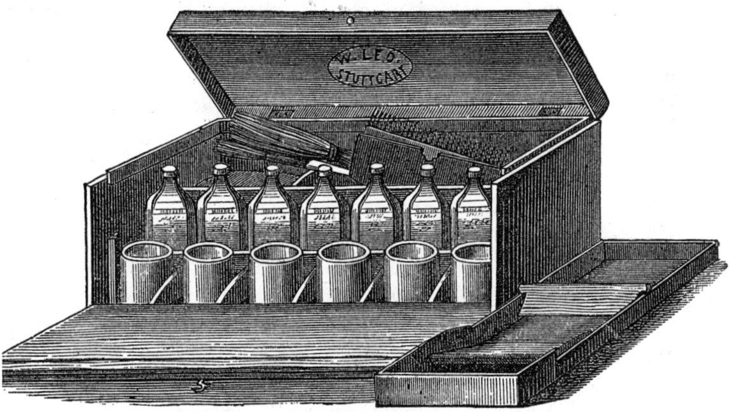

Leo's Marbling Set.

hang it up to dry on a cord; when dry, glaze it, and it is done. You may also embellish your paper with streaks of gold, by applying mussel gold or silver, tempered with gum water, among the rest of the colours."

This last paragraph shows that the gold vein which is now in such demand is really over 150 years old.

Messrs. Leo, of Stuttgart, have put together a complete marbling apparatus, containing colours, gall, cups, combs, sticks, filter, brushes, etc., the whole in a box. To a small country bookbinder this is indispensable.

CHAPTER XVII.

Gilt Edges.

A gilt edge is the most elegant of all modes of ornamenting edges, and this branch of bookbinding has from time to time been so greatly extended, that at the present day there are many ways in which a book may have the edges gilt; but some methods are not pursued, either from ignorance on the binder's part, or with a view to save expense.

First we have the "*plain gilt*," then "*gilt in the round*"; then again some colour under the gold, for instance, "*gilt on red*," or whatever the colour may be, red being mostly used, especially for religious books. Some edges are "*tooled*," and some have a gilt edge with landscape or scene appropriate to the book painted on the edge, only to be seen when the book is opened. "*Marbling under gilt*" may also be used with good effect; but still better "*marbling on gilt*."

The room where gilt edge work is done should be neither dirty nor draughty, and the necessary materials are:—

1*st*. *The Gold Cushion*.—This may be purchased ready for use, or if the binder wishes to make one, it may be done by covering a piece of wood, about 12 inches by 6, with a piece of white calf, the *rough side* outwards, and padding it with blotting paper and cloth. The pieces underneath should be cut a little smaller than the upper one, so that it will form a bevel at the edge, but quite flat on the top. The calf to be neatly nailed all round the edge. If the pile of the leather is too rough, it can be reduced with a piece of pumice stone, by rubbing the stone on the calf with a circular motion.

2nd. *Gold Knife.*—This should be a long knife of thin steel, the blade about one to one and a half inch wide.

3rd. *Burnishers.*—These are made of agate stone, and can be purchased of any size. A flat one, and two or three round ones, will be found sufficient. They should have a very high polish.

4th. *Glaire Water or Size.*—The white of an egg and a tea-cup full of water are well beaten together, until the albumen is perfectly dissolved. It must then be allowed to stand for some hours to settle, after which it should be strained through a piece of linen which has been washed; old linen is therefore preferred to new.

5th. *Scrapers.*—Pieces of steel with the edge or burr made to turn up by rubbing the edge flat over a bodkin or other steel instrument, so that when applied to the edge a thin shaving of paper is taken off. The beauty of gilding depends greatly on proper and even scraping.

6th. *The Gold Leaf.*—This is bought in books, the price according to quality; most of the cheap gold comes from Germany. I recommend the use of the best gold that can be had; it being in the end the cheapest, as cheap gold turns black by the action of the atmosphere in course of time.

The method of preparing the gold[1] is by making an alloy: gold with silver or copper. It is drawn out into a wire of about six inches in length, and by being passed again between steel rollers is made into a ribbon. This ribbon is then cut into squares and placed between vellum leaves, about four or five inches square, and beaten with a hammer somewhat like our beating hammer, until the gold has expanded to the size of the vellum. The gold is again cut up into squares of about one inch, and again inter-

[1] Although this has practically nothing to do with the art of bookbinding, it is always advisable for a workman to know something about the tools and materials he uses.

leaved; but gold-beaters' skin is now used instead of vellum; and so by continual beating and cutting up, the proper thickness is arrived at. If the gold is held up to the light, it will be found to be beaten so thin that it is nearly transparent, although when laid on any object it is of sufficient thickness to hide the surface underneath. It has been estimated that the thickness of the gold leaf is only $\frac{1}{280000}$ of an inch.

To gild the edges, the book should be put into the press straight and on a level with the cheeks of the press between cutting boards, the boards of the book being thrown back. The press should be screwed up very tightly, and any projection of the cutting boards should be taken away with a chisel. If the paper is unsized or at all spongy, the edge should be sized and left to dry. This may be ascertained by wetting a leaf with the tongue: if spongy, the moisture will sink through as in blotting paper. The edge should be scraped quite flat and perfectly even, care being taken to scrape every part equally, or one part of the edge will be hollow or perhaps one side scraped down, and this will make one square larger than the other. When scraped quite smoothly and evenly, a mixture of black lead and thin glaire water is painted over the edge, and with a hard brush it is well brushed until dry.

The gold should now be cut on the gold cushion. Lift a leaf out of the book with the gold knife, lay it on the gold cushion, and breathe gently on the centre of the leaf to lay it flat; it can then be cut with perfect ease to any size. The edge is now to be glaired evenly, and the gold taken up with a piece of paper previously greased by drawing it over the head. The gold is then gently laid on the edge, which has been previously glaired. The whole edge or end being done, it is allowed to get perfectly dry, which will occupy some two hours.

Before using the burnisher on the gold itself, some gilders

lay a piece of fine paper on the gold and gently flatten it with the burnisher. Books are often treated in this manner, they then become " dull gilt." When intended to be bright, a waxed cloth should be gently rubbed over the surface two or three times before using the burnisher. The beauty of burnishing depends upon the edge presenting a solid and uniform metallic surface, without any marks of the burnisher. The manner of burnishing is to hold a flat burnisher, where the surface is flat, firmly in the right hand with the end of the handle on the shoulder, to get better leverage. Work

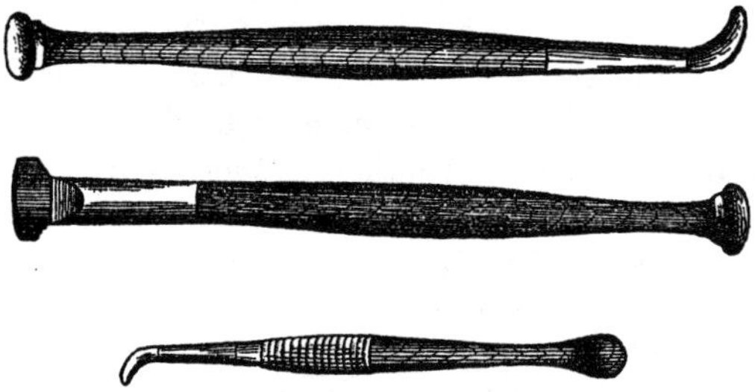

Book-edge Burnishers.

the burnisher backwards and forwards with a perfectly even pressure on every part. When both ends are finished, the foredge is to be proceeded with, by making it perfectly flat. It is better to tie the book, to prevent it slipping back. The foredge is to be gilt exactly in the same manner as the ends; it will of course return to its proper round when released from the press. This is done with all books in the ordinary way, but if the book is to have an extra edge, it is done "solid" or "in the round." For this way the book must be put into the press with its proper round, without flattening it, and scraped in that position with scrapers corresponding with the rounding. The greatest care must be taken in this kind of scraping that the sides are not scraped away, or the squares will be made either too large or lop-sided.

Gilt on Red.—The edges are coloured by fanning them out as explained in colouring edges, and when dry, gilt in the usual way; not quite such a strong size will be wanted, through there being a ground in the colour; nor must any black lead be used. The edges should in this process be scraped first, then coloured and gilt in the usual way.

Tooled Edges.—The book is to be gilt as usual, then while in the press stamped or worked over with tools that are of some open character; those of fine work being preferable. Some design should be followed out according to the fancy of the workman. The tools must be warmed slightly so that the impression may be firm; the foredge should be done first. Another method is to tool the edge before burnishing, or the different portions of the tooling may be so managed in burnishing that some parts will be left bright and standing in relief on the unburnished or dead surface.

Painted Edges.—The edge is to fanned out and tied between boards, and whilst in that position some landscape or other scene, either taken from the book itself or appropriate to the subject of it, painted on the foredge, and when quite dry it is gilt on the flat in the usual manner. This work of course requires an artist well skilled in water-colour drawing. The colours used must be more of a stain than body colour, and the edges should be scraped first.

After the edges have been gilt by any of the foregoing methods, the rounding must be examined and corrected; and the book should be put into the standing press for two or three hours, to set it. The whole of the edges should be wrapped up with paper to keep them clean during the remainder of the process of binding. This is called "capping up."

CHAPTER XVIII.

Head-banding.

Few binders work their own head-bands in these times of competition and strikes for higher wages. It takes some time and pains to teach a female hand the perfection of head-band working, and but too often, since gratitude is not universal, the opportunity of earning a few more pence per week is seized without regard to those at whose expense the power of earning anything was gained, and the baffled employer is wearied by constant changes. Owing to this, most bookbinders use the machine-made head-band. These can be purchased of any size or colour, at a moderate price.

Head-banding done by hand is really only a twist of different coloured cotton or silk round a piece of vellum or cat-gut fastened to the back every half dozen sections. If the head-band is to be square or straight, the vellum should be made by sticking with paste two or three pieces together. Damp the vellum previously and put it under a weight for a few hours to get soft. Vellum from old ledgers and other vellum bound books is mostly used. The vellum when quite dry and flat is to be cut into strips just a little under the width of the squares of the books, so that when the book is covered, the amount of leather above the head-band and the head-band itself will be just the size or height of the square.

If, however, a round head-band is chosen, cat-gut is taken on the same principle with regard to size, and this is further advanced by using two pieces of cat-gut, the one being generally smaller than the other, and making with the beading three rows. The round head-band is the original head-band, and cord was used instead of cat-gut. The cords were fastened to lay-cords on the sewing press, and placed at head and tail, and the head-band was worked at the same time that the book was sewn. I am now speaking of books bound about the 15th century; and in pulling one of these old bindings to pieces, it will compensate for the time occupied and the trouble taken, if the book be examined to see how the head-band was worked, and how the head-band then formed the catch-up stitch; the head-band

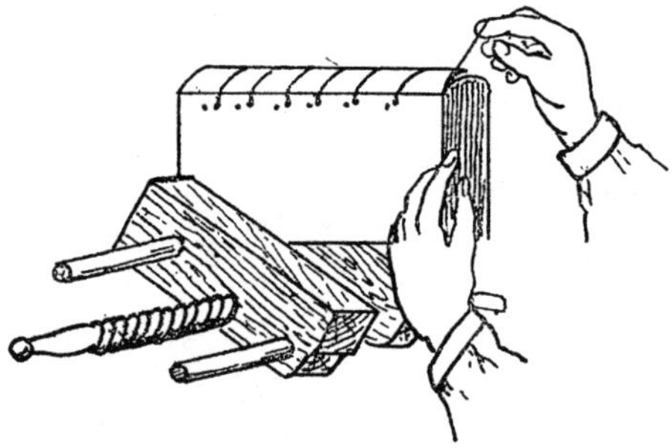

Head-banding.

cords were drawn in through the boards, and thus gave greater strength to the book than the method used at the present day. To explain how the head-band is worked is rather a difficult task; yet the process is a very simple one. The great difficulty is to get the silks to lie close together, which they will not do if the twist or beading is not evenly worked. This requires time and patience to accomplish. The hands must be clean or the silk will get soiled; fingers must be smooth or the silk will be frayed.

Suppose, for instance, a book is to be done in two colours, red and white. The head-band is cut to size, the book is, for convenience, held in a press, or a plough with the knife taken out, so that the end to be head-banded is raised to a convenient height. The ends of the silk or cotton are to be joined together, and one, say the red, threaded through a strong needle. This is then passed through the back of the book, at about the centre of the second section, commencing on the left of the book. This must be passed through twice, and a loop left. The vellum is put in this loop and the silk drawn tightly, the vellum will then be held fast. The white is now to be twisted round the red once, and round the head-band twice; the red is now to be taken in hand and twisted round the white once, and the head-band twice; and this is to be done until the whole vellum is covered. The needle must be passed through the back at about every eight sections to secure the head-band. The beading is the effect of one thread being twisted over the other, and the hand must be kept exactly at the same tightness or tension, for if pulled too tightly the beading will go underneath, or be irregular. The fastening off is to be done by passing the needle through the back twice, the white is then passed round the red and under the vellum, and the ends are to be tied together.

Three Colours Plain.—This is to be commenced in the same way as with two, but great care must be taken that the silks are worked in rotation so as not to mix or entangle them. The silks must be kept in the left hand, while the right twists the colour over or round, and as each is twisted round the vellum it is passed to be twisted round the other two. In fastening off, both colours must be passed round under the vellum and fastened as with the two colour pattern.

The head-bands may be worked intermixed with gold or silver thread, or the one colour may be worked a number of times round the vellum, before the second colour has been twisted, giving it the appearance of ribbons going round the head-band.

With regard to stuck-on head-bands, the binder may make them at little expense, by using striped calico for the purpose. A narrow stripe is to be preferred of some bright colour. The material must be cut into lengths of about one-and-a-half inch wide, with the stripes across. Cords of different thickness are then to be cut somewhat longer than the calico, and a piece of the cord is to be fastened by a nail at one end on a board of sufficient length. The calico is then to be pasted and laid down on the board under the cord, and the cord being held tightly may be easily covered with the striped calico, and rubbed with a folder into a groove.

When this is dry, the head and tail of the book is glued and the proper piece of the head-band is put on. Or the head-band may be purchased, as before stated, worked with either silk or cotton ready for fastening on, from about 2*s.* 3*d.* to 4*s.* 6*d.* a piece of twelve yards, according to the size required: it has, however, the disadvantage of not looking so even as a head-band worked on the book. I have lately seen some specimens of as good imitations of hand-worked ones as it is possible for machinery to manufacture.

After the head-band has been put on or worked, the book is to be "lined up" or "made ready for covering."

CHAPTER XIX.

Preparing for Covering.

Nearly all modern books are bound with hollow backs, except where the books are sewn for flexible work or otherwise meant to have tight backs.

Much of the paper used at the present day is so hard, that the binder is almost forced to make a hollow back, in order that the book may open.

The head-band is first set with glue, if worked, by gluing the head and tail, and with a folder the head-band is made to take the same form as the back. This is to be done by holding the book in the left hand with its back on the press, then a pointed folder held in the right hand is run round the beading two or three times to form it; the silk on the back is then rubbed down as much as possible to make all level and even, and the book is allowed to dry. When dry it is put into the lying press to hold it, and the back is well glued all over; some paper, usually brown, is now taken, the same length as the book, put on the back, and rubbed down well with a thick folder: a good sized bone from the ribs of beef is as good as anything. The overplus of the paper is now to be cut away from the back, except the part projecting head and tail. A second coat of glue is now put on the top of the brown paper and another piece is put on that, but not quite up to the edge on the left hand side. When this is well rubbed down it is folded evenly from the edge on the right side over to the left, the small amount of glued space left will be found sufficient to hold it down; the top is again glued and again folded over from left to right, and cut off level by folding it back and running a sharp knife down the fold. This is what is generally termed "two on and two off," being of course two thicknesses of paper on the back and two for the hollow; but thin or small books need only have one on the back and two for the hollow. Thick or large books should have more paper used in proportion to their size. Books that have been over-cast in the sewing should have rather a strong lining-up, so that there be not such a strain when the book is opened. When the whole is dry, the overplus of the paper, head and tail, is to be cut off close to the head-band.

I need hardly say that the better the paper used the more easy will be the working of it. Old writing or copy-book paper will be found to be as good as any, but good brown paper is, as I have said before, mostly used.

The book is now ready for putting the bands on. These are prepared beforehand by sticking with glue two or three pieces of leather together or on a piece of paper, well pressing it, and then allowing it to dry under pressure. The paper must then be glued twice, allowing each coat to dry before gluing again. It should then be put on one side for future use, and when wanted, the proper thickness is chosen and cut into strips of a width to correspond with the size of the book. The book is now to be marked up, five bands being the number generally used, leaving the tail a little longer than the other portions. The strips of band are then to be moistened with a little hot water to cause the glue upon the paper to melt. Each piece is then to be fixed upon the back just under the holes made with the compasses in marking-up. This will be found to be a far better plan than to first cut the strips and then to glue them. By the latter plan the glue is liable to spread upon the side, where it is not wanted, and if the book has to be covered with light calf, it will certainly be stained black:

so the coverer must be careful that *all glue is removed* from the back and sides before he attempts to cover any of his books with calf. It is rather provoking to find some favourite colour when dry, having a tortoiseshell appearance, which no amount of washing will take out. When dry the ends of the bands are to be cut off with a *bevel*, and a little piece of the boards from the corners nearest the back also taken off on the bevel, that there may not be a sharp point to fret through the leather when the book is opened. This is also necessary so that the head-band may be properly set. A sharp knife should be inserted between the hollow and should separate it from the back at head and tail on each side so far as to allow the leather to be turned in. Morocco may have the back glued, as it will not show through, and will facilitate the adhesion of the leather.

Flexible Work.—This class of work is not lined-up. The leather is fastened directly upon the book; the head-band is set as before explained, and held tight by gluing a piece of fine linen against it, and when quite dry, the overplus is to be cut away, and the back made quite smooth. The bands are then knocked up gently with a blunt chisel to make them perfectly straight, being first damped and made soft with a little paste to facilitate the working and to prevent the thread from being cut. Any holes caused by sawing-in, in previous binding, must be filled up with a piece of frayed cord, pasted. Any holes thus filled up must be made quite smooth when dry, as the least unevenness will show when the book is covered.

In "throw up" backs, or in "flexible not to show," a piece of thin linen (muslin) or stuff called *mull* is glued on the back first, and one piece of paper on the top. For the hollow, three, four, or even five pieces are stuck one on the other, so that it may be firm; whilst the book itself will be as if it had a flexible back. The bands, if any, are then to be fastened on, and the corners of the boards cut off. It is then ready for covering. "Mock flexible" has generally one piece of paper glued on the back, and when marked-up, the bands are put on as before, and the book covered.

CHAPTER XX.

COVERING.

BOOKS are covered according to the fancy of the binder or customer. The materials used at the present day, are—leather of all sorts, parchment or vellum, bookbinder's cloth, velvet, needle-work, and imitation leather, of which various kinds are manufactured, such as leatherette and feltine.

Each kind requires a different manner of working or manipulation. For instance, a calf book must not be covered in the same manner as a velvet one: I will take each in the above order and explain how they are managed.

Under the class of leather, we have moroccos of all kinds; russia; calf, coloured, smooth, and imitation; roan, sheep, and imitation morocco.

The *morocco* cover, indeed any leather cover, is to be cut out by laying the skin out on a flat board, and having chosen the part or piece of the skin to be used, the book is laid on it and the skin is cut with a sharp knife round the book, leaving a space of about ¾ of an inch for an 8vo, and more or less according to the size of the book and thickness of board for turning in. The morocco

French Paring Knife.

cover should now have marked upon it with a pencil the exact size of the book itself, by laying the book on the cover, and running the point of a black lead pencil all round it. The leather must then be "pared," or shaved round the edges, using the pencil marks as a guide. This paring process is *not* so difficult, especially if a French knife is used, such as may now be purchased at most material dealers. The chief point being that a very sharp edge is to be kept on the knife, and that the *burr* is on the cutting edge. The knife is to be held in the right hand, placing two fingers on the top with the thumb underneath. The leather must be placed on a piece of marble, lithographic stone, or thick glass, and held tightly strained between finger and thumb of the left hand. Then by a series of pushes from the right hand, the knife takes off more or less according to the angle given. The burr causes the knife to enter the leather; if the burr is turned up the knife will not cut but run off.

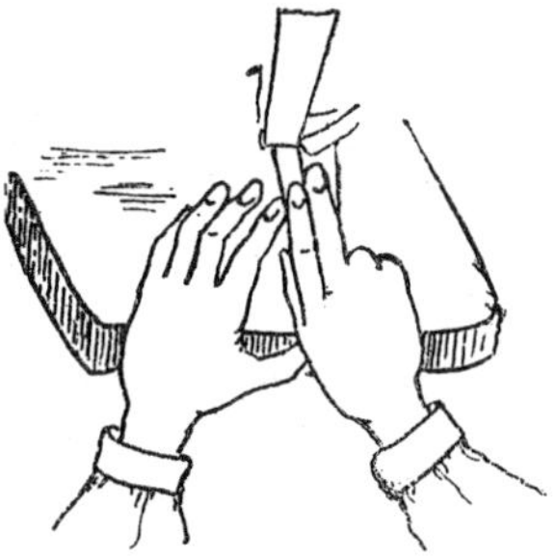

Method of Holding French Knife.

German Paring Knife.

If the knife is held too much at an angle it will go right through the leather, a rather unpleasant experience, and one to be carefully avoided. The leather should from time to time be examined, by turning it over, to see if any unevenness appears, for every cut will show. Especial attention should be given to where the edges of the board go. The turning in at the head and tail should be pared off as thin as possible, as there will be twice as much thickness of leather on the back where turned in, the object of this care being, that it must not be seen. The *morocco* cover should now be wetted well, and grained up by using either the hand or a flat piece of cork. This is to be done by gently curling it up in all directions; and when the grain has been brought up properly and sufficiently, the leather should be pasted on the flesh side with thin paste, and hung up to dry. Should the leather be "straight grain," it must only be creased in the one direction of the grain, or if it is required to imitate any old book that has no grain, the leather should be wetted as much as possible, and the whole of the grain rubbed out by using a rolling pin with even pressure.

The Morocco leather first brought from *that* country, had

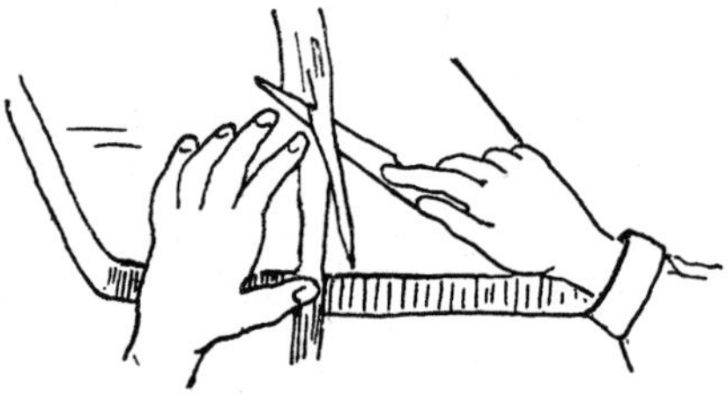

Method of Holding Ordinary Knife.

a peculiar grain, and was dyed with very bright colours. It is now largely manufactured in London and Paris; the French manufacture is the finest. Russia and calf require no setting up of the grain, but russia should be well rolled out with the rolling pin.

When the cover (morocco) is dry, it is to be well pasted, the squares of the book set, so that each side has its proper portion of board projecting. The book is then laid down evenly on the cover, which must be gently drawn on; the back is drawn tight by placing the book on its foredge and drawing the skin well down over it. The sides are next drawn tight, and the bands pinched well up with a pair of *band nippers*. The four corners of the leather are cut off with a sharp knife in a slanting direction, a little paste put on the cut edge, and the operation of turning in may be commenced. The book must be held on its edge, either head or tail, with a small piece of paper put close to the head-band to prevent any paste soiling the edge or head-band, and with the boards extended, the hollow is pulled a little away from the back and the leather neatly tucked in. The leather is next to be tightly brought over the boards and well rubbed down, both on the edge and inside, with a folding stick, but on no account must the outside be rubbed, or the grain will be taken away. The foredge is to be treated in like manner, by tucking the corners in for strength. The head-band is now to be set, by tying a piece of thread round the book between the back and the boards in the slots cut out from the corners of the boards; this thread must be tied in a knot. The book being held in the left hand, resting on its end, the leather is drawn with a pointed folding-stick, as it were, towards the foredge, and flattened on the top of the head-band. When this is done properly it should be exactly even with the boards, and yet *cover* the head-band, leaving that part of the head-band at right angles with the edge exposed. With a little practice the novice may be able to ascertain what amount of leather is to be left out from the turning-in, so that the head-band can be neatly covered. The perfection in covering a book depends upon the leather being worked sharp round the boards, but with the grain almost untouched.

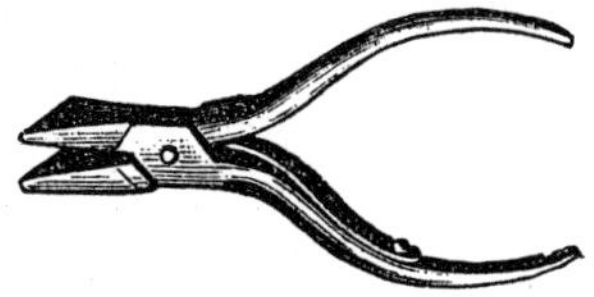

Band Nippers.

Paste should be always used for morocco, calf, russia and vellum, in fact for all kinds of leather; but in my humble opinion, all leather with an artificial grain should be glued; the turning-in may be with paste. The glue gives more body to the leather, and thus preserves the grain. *White* morocco should be covered with paste made *without any alum*, which causes it to turn *yellow*, and if the leather is washed with lemon juice instead of vinegar when finishing, the colour will be much improved.

Russia is to be pared in the same way as morocco. It should be damped, and rolled with a rolling-pin before covering, or stretched out with a thick folding-stick.

Calf, either coloured or white, need be pared only round the head-band. Calf should be covered with paste and the book washed when covered with a clean damp sponge. In putting two books together, when bound in calf of two different colours, a piece of paper should be placed between, as most colours stain each other, especially green. Care should be taken to handle calf as little as possible whilst wet, and touching it with iron tools, such as knives and band nippers, will cause a black stain. Morocco will bear as much handling as you like, but the more tenderly calf is treated the better.

Vellum or Parchment.—The boards should be covered with white paper, to avoid any darkness of the board showing through. The vellum or parchment should be pared head and tail, and the whole well pasted and allowed to stand for a short time so that it be well soaked and soft. The book should then be covered, but the vellum must not on any account be stretched much, or it will, when dry, draw the boards up to a most remarkable extent. It will perhaps be better if the book be pressed, to make the vellum adhere better. The old binders took great pains in covering their white vellum books. The vellum was lined carefully with white paper and dried before covering: this in some degree prevented the vellum from shrinking so much in drying, and enabled the workman to give the boards a thin and even coat of glue, which was allowed to dry before putting on the covering.

Roan should be covered with glue and turned in with paste. Head and tail only need be pared round the head-band.

Cloth is covered by gluing the cover all over and turning in at once: gluing one cover at a time, and finishing the covering of each book before touching the next.

Smooth cloth, cloth with no grain, may be covered with paste: great care must be taken that no paste be on the fingers, or the cloth will be marked very badly when dry.

Velvet should be covered with clean glue not too thick; first glue the *back* of the book and let that set before the sides are put down. The sides of the *book* should next be glued, and the velvet laid down, and turned in with glue. The corners should be very carefully cut or they will not meet, or cover properly when dry. When the whole is dry the pile may be raised, should it be finger marked, by holding the book over steam, and if necessary by carefully using a brush.

Silk and Satin should be lined first with a piece of thin paper cut to the size of the book. The paper must be glued with thin clean glue, rubbed down well on to the silk, and allowed to get dry, before covering the book. When dry, cover it as with velvet.

Dr. Dibdin, whose knowledge of libraries and great book collectors must stamp him as an authority, says that:—

"The general appearance of one's library is by no means a matter of mere foppery or indifference: it is a sort of cardinal point, to which the tasteful collector does well to attend. You have a right to consider books, as to their outsides, with the eye of a painter; because this does not militate against the proper use of the contents. . . . . Be sparing of red morocco or vellum, they have each so distinct, or what painters call spotty, an appearance, that they should be introduced but circumspectly."

I cannot agree entirely with the Doctor with regard to being sparing with the red morocco. A library without colour is dark, dreary, and repulsive. The library should be one of the most inviting and cheery rooms in a house, and even if one cannot aspire to a room entirely devoted to literature and study, let the bookcase, whatever its position or however humble, be made as cheerful and inviting as possible. What colour will do this so well as red? But it should be judiciously dispersed with other colours.

If some standard colour were chosen for each subject, one might recognize from some little distance the nature of the book by its colour. For instance, all books relating to Military matters might be in bright red; Naval affairs in blue; Botany in green; History in dark red; Poetry in some fancy colour, such as orange, light blue, light green, or olive, according to its subject; Divinity in dark brown; Archæology in dull red, and Law in white as at present. This would give a pleasing variety, and a light and cheerful appearance to a library.

An imitation russia leather is imported from America, of far greater strength than the real. It is made from buffalo skins, and tanned in the same way as the russia hides. This fact, combined with the price, has doubtless caused this material to be received with favour in the English market. It is to be had from nearly all leather sellers.

Half-bound Work.—The title speaks for itself, the book has its back, a part of the sides, and the corners covered with leather. The sides are, after the leather is perfectly dry, covered either with cloth or paper according to fancy, turned over the boards as with leather. The book is then to be pasted down. Before the paper is put on the sides, all unevenness of the leather is to be pared away. This style has gained its reputation very much on account of its economy; the amount of leather required is less, and the work is as strong and serviceable as in a whole-bound book. It will be better if the back be finished before the corners are put on, as there is great likelihood that the corners may get damaged to some extent during the process of finishing. The outside paper may either match the colour of the leather, or be the same as the edge or end papers. This, like many other rules in bookbinding, is quite a matter of taste.

CHAPTER XXI.

Pasting Down.

This is to cover up the inside board by pasting down the end papers to the boards.

The white or waste leaf, that has till this process protected the end papers, must now be taken away or torn out. The joint of the board must be cleaned of any paste or glue that may have accumulated there during the course of either gluing up or covering, by passing the point of a sharp knife along it, so that when the end is pasted down, the joint will be quite straight and perfectly square. Morocco books should be filled in with a smooth board or thick paper, the exact substance of the leather. This thickness must be carefully chosen, and one edge be cut off straight, and fastened to the inside of the board very slightly, in fact only touching it in the centre with a little glue or paste, just sufficient to hold it temporarily. It must be flush with the back-edge of the board. When dry, this paper or board is to be marked with a compass about half an inch round, and both paper and leather cut through at the same cut with a sharp knife. The overplus board will fall off and the outside of the leather may be easily detached by lifting it up with a knife. The paper or board, which will now fit in exactly, should be glued and well rubbed down with a folding stick, or it may be pressed in the standing press if the grain of the morocco is to be polished, but not otherwise.

As morocco books only have morocco joints, I may as well explain at once how they are made. Morocco of the same colour is cut into strips the same length as the book, and about one inch and a half in breadth for 8vo.; a line is drawn or marked down each strip about half an inch from one edge, either with a pencil or folder, as a guide. The leather is now to be pared from the mark made to a thin edge on the half inch side, and the other side pared as thin as the leather turned in round the board, so that there will be two distinct thicknesses on each piece, the larger half going on the board to correspond with the leather round the three sides, and the smaller and thinly pared half going in the joint and edge on to the book. The end papers, only held in with a little paste, are to be lifted out from the book, and the leather well pasted is to be put on the board, so that the place where the division is made in the leather by paring will come exactly to the edge of the board; the thin part should then be well rubbed down in the joint, and the small thin feather edge allowed to go on the book.

Great care must be taken to rub the whole down well, that it may adhere properly; the grain need not be heeded. With regard to the overplus at the head and tail, there are two ways of disposing of it: first, by cutting both leathers slanting through at once, and making the two meet; or, secondly, by cutting the cover away in a slant and doing the same to the joint, so that the two slant cuts cover each other exactly. This requires very nice paring, or it will be seen in the finishing. The book should be left till quite dry, which will take some five or six hours. The boards are then to be filled in by the same method as above described, and the end papers fastened in again properly.

Cloth Joints.—If the cloth has been fastened in when the ends were made, after cleaning all unevenness from the joints, the boards are to be filled in as above, and the cloth joint stuck down with thin glue, and rubbed down well. The marble paper may now be put on the board by cutting it to a size a little larger than the filling in of the board, so that it may be well covered. When cloth joints are put in, the board paper is generally brought up almost close to the joint; but with morocco joints, the space left all round should be even.

Calf, Russia, etc.—After having cleaned the joint, the leather must be marked all round a trifle larger than the size intended for the end papers to cover. Then with a knife, the leather is cut through in a *slanting direction* by holding the knife slanting. The boards should be thrown back to protect the leather, and the book placed on a board of proper size, so that both book and board may be moved together, when turning round. When the leather is cut, a piece of paper should be pasted on the board to fill up to the thickness of the leather, and to curve or swing the board back; the boards otherwise are sure to curve the contrary way, especially with calf. When this lining is dry, the end papers may be pasted down. As there are two methods of doing this, I give the most exact but longest first. The paper is to be pasted all over, and being held in the left hand, is to be well rubbed down, particularly in the joint. The paper is then marked all round—the head, foredge, and tail, with a pair of compasses to the width required for finishing inside the board. With a very sharp knife the paper is to be cut through to the *depth* of the *paper only*, by laying the straight edge on the marks made by the compasses. This has the advantage of procuring an exact margin round the board, but it must be done quickly or the paper will stick to the leather round the board from the paste getting dry, the leather absorbing the watery particles in the paste.

The other way is to lay the paper back, and down on the board, and then to mark it. A tin is then to be placed between the book and paper, and the paper cut to the marks made. The paper is then pasted down as above. When pasted down, the book should be left standing on its end, with boards left open until thoroughly dry, which will be about six hours. A tin should be kept especially for cutting on, and the knife must be as sharp as possible. This latter method is used for all half bindings.

CHAPTER XXII.

Calf Colouring.

Although coloured calf-skins may be bought almost as cheaply as smooth calf (the term given to uncoloured ones), yet there are so many reasons why coloured calf should not be used, that I give such instructions as will enable any one to colour, sprinkle, and marble his own leather.

The skins may, however, be procured already sprinkled or marbled at most leather shops. This plan of sprinkling and marbling the whole skin is good enough for cheap or half-bound work, but for extra work it is far better to sprinkle, marble, or otherwise colour the leather when on the book. Hand-colouring is coming again into use, and by degrees getting known more and more throughout the trade; but a great many secrets in the art have been lost. Before giving the names of the chemicals to be used, I must give a general caution, that if any acid be used on the leather, it is essential to wash as much as possible of it out with water *immediately after it has done its work*, or after a few months the surface of the leather will be found to be eaten away and destroyed. It is a fault of some of our binders at the present day, that if they use any chemical, either on their leather or on their paper, they are not satisfied to use their acid weak, and allow it to do its work slowly, and when the proper moment has arrived stop its further action, they frequently use the acids as strong as possible, and, either to save time or through ignorance of their chemical properties, do not wash out the residue. The consequence is, the leather or the paper rots. In order to avoid this, I will not recommend any chemicals that will destroy the leather, but give instructions for harmless preparations, by the use of which as great a variety of different styles may be executed as will, I trust, satisfy any reasonable expectation.

Black.—Sulphate of iron or copperas is the chief ingredient in colouring calf black. Used by itself, it gives a greyish tint, but if a coat of salts of tartar or other alkali be previously used it strikes immediately a rich purple black. The name copperas is probably from the old and mistaken idea that the crystals contain copper. They have a pale greenish blue colour. It can be purchased at the rate of one penny per pound from any drysalter.

1. Into a quart of boiling water, throw a ¼-lb. of sulphate of iron, let it re-boil, and stand to settle, and then bottle the clear liquid for use.

2. Boil a quart of vinegar with a quantity of old iron nails or steel filings for a few minutes. Keep this in a stone jar, and use the clear liquid. This can from time to time be boiled again with fresh vinegar. An old iron pot must be kept for boiling the black.

Brown.—1. Dissolve a $\frac{1}{4}$-lb. of salts of tartar in a quart of boiling water, and bottle it for use.

This liquid is mostly used for colouring; it has a very mellow tone, and is always used before the black when a strong or deep colour is required. It is poisonous, and must not be used too strong on the calf or it will corrode it.

2. For a plain brown dye, the green shells of walnuts may be used. They should be broken as much as possible, mixed with water, and allowed to ferment. This liquid should then be strained and bottled for use. A pinch of salt thrown in will help to keep it. This does not in any way corrode the leather, and produces the best uniform tint.

Yellow.—1. Picric acid dissolved in water forms one of the sharpest yellows. It is a pale yellow of an intense bitter taste. It must not be mixed with any alkali in a dry state, as it forms a very powerful explosive compound. It is a dangerous chemical and should be carefully used. It may be bottled for use.

2. Into a bottle put some turmeric powder, and mix well with methylated spirit; the mixture must be shaken occasionally for a few days until the whole of the colour is extracted. This is a very warm yellow, and produces a very good shade when used after salts of tartar.

For all the following, a preparation or ground of paste-water must be put on the calf, that the liquids may not sink through too much. The calf must be paste-washed all over equally, and allowed to get thoroughly dry. It will then be ready for the various methods. Perhaps to wash it over night and let it stand till next morning will be the best and surest plan. It matters very little whether the calf is on the book or in the skin.

Sprinkles.—There are so many sprinkles, that it would be useless for me to enumerate a number, they are all worked in the same manner, by throwing the colour on finely or coarsely, as it may be wanted light or dark.

Presuming that the paste or ground-wash be thoroughly dry, take liquid salts of tartar and dilute with cold water, one part salts to two of water, in a basin; wash the calf with this liquid evenly, using a soft sponge. The calf will require the wash to be applied two or three times, until a proper and uniform tint be obtained. Each successive wash must be allowed to get thoroughly dry before the next be applied.

The next process will be to sprinkle the book, with the boards extended or open. Two pieces of flat wood, about three feet long, four inches in width, and half an inch thick, will be found very useful for supporting the book. These rods must be supported at each end, so that the book may be suspended between them, with the boards resting on the rods nearly horizontally. Now put into a round pan some of the copperas fluid, and into another some of the solution of salts of tartar. Use a pretty large brush for each pan, which brush must be kept each for its own fluid. The sprinkling may be commenced. The brushes being well soaked in the fluids, should be well beaten out, using a piece of broomstick or a hand pin to beat on before beating over the book, unless a coarse sprinkle is desired. Whilst beating over the book, the hands should be held up high, and also moved about, so that a fine and equal spray may be distributed; and this should be continued until the desired depth of colour is attained.

This may be varied by putting some geometrical design, cut out of thin mill-board, on the cover; or if the book is on any special subject, the subject itself put on the cover will have a very pretty effect, and may be made emblematical. A fern or other leaf for botanical work as an instance. The sprinkle must in these cases be very fine and dark for the better effect. The leaf or design being lifted from the cover when the sprinkle is dry, will leave the ground dark sprinkle with a light brown leaf or design. *Cambridge calf* is done in this way by cutting a square panel of mill-board out and laying it on the sides. The square on the cover may be left brown or may be dabbed with a sponge.

Marbles.—As the success of marbling depends upon the quickness with which it is executed, it is important that the colours, sponges, brushes and water, should be previously disposed in order and at hand, so that any of them can be taken up instantly. Another point to which attention must be directed is the amount of colour to be thrown on, and consequently the amount that each brush should contain. If too much colour (black) is thrown on, the result will be an invisible marble, or, as I once heard it expressed by a workman, "it could not be seen on account of the fog;" if too little, no matter how nicely the marble is formed, it will be weak and feeble.

Marbling on leather is produced by small drops of colouring liquids, drawn, by the flowing of water down an inclined plane, into veins and spread into fantastic forms resembling foliage—hence, often called *tree-marble.* It is a process that requires great dexterity of hand and perfect coolness and decision, as the least hurry or want of judgment will ruin the most elaborate preparation.

To prepare the book paste-wash it evenly all over, and to further equalize the paste-water, pass the palm of the hand over the board after washing it. When dry, wash over with a solution of salts of tartar two or three times to get the desired tint. When dry, glaire the whole as even as possible, and to diminish the froth that the sponge may occasion, put a few drops of milk into the glaire. Again allow it to dry thoroughly. Put some fresh copperas into a pan, and some solution of salts of tartar into another, and soak each brush in its liquid. Place the book upon the rods, the boards extending over and the book hanging between. Should it be desired to let the marble run from back to foredge the back must be elevated a little, and the rods supporting the boards must be level from end to end. If the marble is to run from head to tail, elevate the ends of the rods nearest to the head of the book. The elevation must be very slight or the water will run off too quickly.

Place a pail of water close at hand, in it a sponge to wash off; and a bunch of birch to throw the water with. A little soda should be added to soften the water. Charge each brush well, and knock out the superfluous colour until a fine spray comes from it. A little oil rubbed in the palm of the hand, and the brush well rubbed into it, will greatly assist the flow of colour from the brush, and also prevent the black colour from frothing. Throw some water over the cover in blotches with the birch, just sufficient to make them unite and flow downwards together. Now sprinkle some black by beating the black brush on a press pin, as evenly and as finely as possible. When sufficient has been thrown on, beat the brown in like manner over the extended boards. When the veins are well struck into the leather, sponge the whole well with clean water. Have no fear in doing this as it will not wash off. Then set the book up to dry.

Tree-marbles.—The cover is to be prepared and sprinkled in the same manner as stated in marbling; the boards, however, must be bent a little, and a little water applied by a sponge in the centre of each board to give the necessary flow of water; when the water is thrown on, it will flow towards the centre or lowest part of the boards, and when the sprinkle is thrown on, a *tree*, as it were, will be formed. The centre being white forms the stem, and from it branches will be formed by the gradual flow of the streams of water as they run down.

For marbling, every thing must be ready at hand before any water is thrown on, so that the water may not have time to run off before the colour is applied. The water must run at the same time that the spray is falling, or a failure will be the result.

It has been said that marbling was discovered by an accident; that a country bookbinder was sprinkling some books, when a bird, which was hung up in the shop, threw or splashed some water down on his books; the water running, took some of the colour with it and formed veins. Liking the form it gave, the workman improved upon it and thus invented marbling. There is, however, no doubt that it had its origin in Germany.

Tree calf seems to be coming into general use again, and to meet the demand for cheapness, a wood block has been cut resembling as closely as possible one done by the water process, and blocked in black on the calf; but, as might have been expected, it has not found much favour.

Dabs.—This is a process with a sponge, charged with the black or the brown liquid, dabbed on the calf either all over the cover or in successive order. Give the proper preparation to the calf, and be very careful that the ground tint of brown be very even. Take a sponge of an open nature, so that the grain is pleasant to the eye; fill it with black and squeeze out again, now dab it carefully over the calf. Repeat the operation with another sponge charged with brown. Cat's paw, French dab, and other various named operations all emanate from the sponge. When done properly this has a very good effect, and gives great relief to the eye when placed with a number of other books.

All these marbles and sprinkles require practice, so that

a first failure must not be regarded with discouragement. When one's hand has got into the method with these two or three colours it is astonishing how many different styles may be produced. In all this manipulation a better effect is obtained if a yellow tint be washed over the leather after the sprinkle or marble has been produced. Again, by taking *coloured calf* and treating it in the same manner as white, some very pleasant effects are brought out; and when the colours are well chosen the result is very good. Take for instance a green calf and marble a tree upon it, or take a light slate colour and dab it all over with black and brown.

In all operations with the copperas care must be taken that it does not get on the clothes, as it leaves an iron stain that cannot be easily got rid of. Keep a bason for each colour, and when done with wash it out with clean water. The same with the sponges: keep them as clean as possible; have a sponge for each colour, and use it only for that colour. A piece of glass to put the sponges on will be of great use, and prevent the work-table or board from catching any of the colour. A damp book or damp paper laid on a board that has been so stained will most probably be damaged, even though it has waste paper between the work-board and book. No amount of washing will ever take away such a stain.

When the book has been coloured, the edges and inside are to be blacked or browned according to taste, or in keeping with the outside. The book is then ready for finishing.

Some very good results may be obtained if the binder, using coloured calf of a light brown, treats it as if it were white calf, marbling with the usual colours; or a yellow calf, splashing it all over with salts of tartar only, the boards being placed in a slanting direction to allow the colour to gently run down.

Or the whole of a cover may be blacked with tartar and copperas, then with a diluted solution of acid it may be sprinkled, this will give grey-white spots on black or slate ground : if, after washing, the cover be sponged over with some colouring liquid, such as analine dyes, the spots will be of the colour used.

I do not give many methods or receipts for producing colours for calf, because, as before stated, the introduction of fancy calf has rendered obsolete the old-fashioned way of boiling and preparing the different woods for making colours, and the above will be found useful for colouring calf in many different ways.

PART II.

FINISHING.

RENAISSANCE.

Roy folio

CHAPTER XXIII.

FINISHING.

FINISHING is the art of embellishing the covers of books with different designs. Finishing comprises the embellishment of the covers either with blind work, gold, silver or platina leaf, or with metal ornaments fastened through the boards, or by only a lettering on the back of the book.

The art of finishing does not comprise any embellishment done with the "blocking press." Therein the art is more that of the block or tool cutter, who, working in concert with the artist who drew the design, cuts the metal accordingly. The binder's use of these blocks is mechanical only.

The monks who cultivated all the arts, and enriched their *Hours* and their *Missals* with marvellous miniatures, gave great zeal to the occupation of binding. So charmingly were the bindings ornamented with tools and small blocks reproduced from the text, that we must regret that so few of these monastic bindings are now left to us.

A great number of these books were executed in Germany, where this mode of decoration remained a long time in use; and we find that other countries borrowed from the printer this primitive mode of decoration. As the art progressed the binder's mark was impressed on the cover as an ornament, or as a distinction, such as we find at the present day at the end or after the title of books to denote by what printer the work was executed. Later on, when the Renaissance shone in all its glory and beauty, we find that it freed itself from this limited practice. A new mode of decoration came into use, which we may well study, even at the present day; a style at once rich and varied. If we follow the bold interlacing lines which form the skeletons of those infinite and varied designs, we catch the imaginative caprices of their authors; and the details of their transformation gives us a guide to the different schools and art of their time. The execution of these linear designs is extremely difficult. It can be easily seen that they have not been done by a block engraved in one piece, but with small segments.[1] The art of putting together these small pieces, so as to form one complete and artistic pattern, is the skill of the *finisher*. Many books are now finished by means of the blocking press; but on close examination, these imitations may be readily distinguished. A blocked cover never has the life and spirit that a hand-finished one has. Of blocking I must speak in subsequent pages.

Monastic Tools.

These intrinsic designs were very much used by the

[1] There are a few exceptions to this on a few old books of 12mo. size. One may now and then see such designs worked in one piece certainly by a block.

ANTIQUE WITH GOLD LINE.

Imperial 8vo.

binders contemporary with *Grolier*, and the use of lined or azuré tools are a distinctive mark of the period. This is

Venetian.

the connecting link with the Italian bindings. It will be observed that the Italian or Venetian tools are solid,

Grolier.

while in the other style the tools, although of the same shape, are lined or azuré. A little later on other artists, not satisfied with this modification, dispensed with the fine cross lines, and retained their outlines only. France, during the reign of Henry II., left Italy far behind, and executed those grand compositions of *Diane* bindings. They are marvellous subjects, and are sometimes imitated at the present day, but are never surpassed in their wonderful originality.

After these masterpieces we find the curious bindings of Henry III., which instantly mark a distinct transformation. The interlacings are less bold and free, but more geometrically traced. The absence of filling in with small tools gives a coldness, which is increased by a heavy coat of

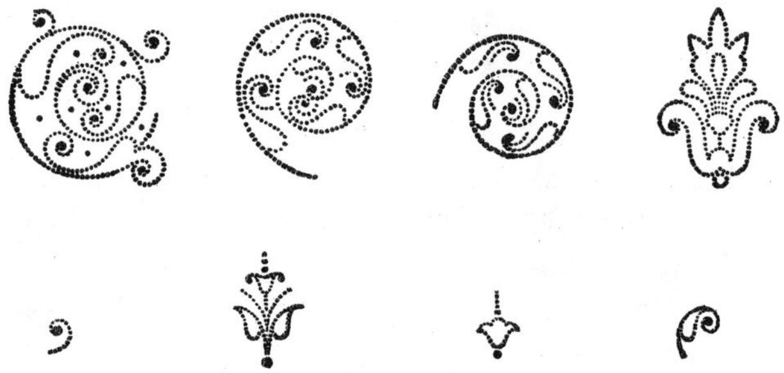

Le Gascon.

arms on the sides. This form of decoration exercised a great influence, and from this epoch another school sprung up. Later on in time these interlacings served as a ground plan only for the brilliant fantasies of *Le Gascon*, a master who no doubt has had the least number of imitators. Although he followed and to a certain extent kept the shapes, the aspect of his bindings was very much changed by the application of pointed tools. *Le Gascon* rests for ever as the most renowned master of the 16th century. The number of tools necessary for the execution of a composition like one of *Le Gascon's* is large; and when one considers that these tools are repeated, perhaps a thousand

DEROME.

4to

times on each side of the book, a fair idea may be formed of the magnitude of such a work. I am of opinion that *Le Gascon* brought bookbinding to its highest point of richness and finish. His drawings are always pure and correct; his squares, lozenges, triangles, and ovals are so brought together as to form a series of compartments interlacing the one within the other, with an incomparable boldness and perfect harmony; above all, one must remark with what richness the compartments are filled. There is no doubt the ground work of the style was *Grolier*, but he

Derome.

never filled his panels with such richness or with such taste as that displayed by *Le Gascon.* The difficulty of adapting such designs to the different sizes of books has no doubt deterred the various masters from imitating such works, so that we see less of *Le Gascon's* style than of any other ancient master.

From *Le Gascon's* period the tools became thicker and thicker, until we have the heavy tools of *Derome*, which are much in keeping for books of a serious character. They are original in shape, but their employment was only in borders, leaving the centre of the book free from ornament.

I do not pretend to give a history of the various masters, but rather a practical description of the art of bookbinding. Much has already been written about the various works executed by these grand old masters; my endeavour has been to show, that whilst the various masters of the art of bookbinding worked with tools but little altered from their original forms, they so modified and changed them in their character and use, as to form a distinctive mark of style for each artist, by which his work may be recognized.

A pamphlet, published in Paris, 1878, says: "One of the branches of artistic industry in which France possesses unquestionable superiority is certainly bookbinding; the International Exhibitions, and still more the sales of private or other collections, have each day given evident proof of this. Italy, which initiated herself so perfectly in the Renaissance style, and Holland, once her rival in the 17th century, have long ceased to produce any work worthy of remark; everywhere books are being bound, but the 'art' of bookbinding is practised only in France."

I cannot agree with its authors that one must go to France now to have a book bound properly. The method of bookbinding is quite differently managed and worked there than it is here. I have witnessed both methods, and prefer the English one as being more substantial.

HAND-FINISHING.—We were first taught to work the gold leaf on books by a method not now employed, except, perhaps, by a novice, who wishes to get his books done before his glaire has dried. This method was to damp the cover well with water, either with a wet sponge or by other means. The gold leaf was then laid on, and the tool worked rather warm on the gold. Through the heat or steam generated the gold was burnt in, and the overplus washed off with a damp sponge or rag, the gold being left only in the impressions. If, however, any block or centre was used, it was impressed with heat upon the side in a small lying press in use at the period. This press was known then as an *arming press*, because used commonly for impressing armorial bearings and monograms on the sides. The term arming press is still used for the lighter kinds of blocking presses.

Hand-finishing, as before stated, is really an *art*. The finisher should be able to draw, or at least have some knowledge of composition, and also know something about the harmony of colours. The workman not having any knowledge of drawing cannot expect to be a good finisher; because he cannot possibly produce any good designs, or by a combination of the small tools form a perfect and correct pattern. Taste has no small influence in the success of the workman in this branch of the art. It is better to finish books plainly, rather than put on the least portion of gold more than is necessary. If the intentions of the books' owner is to put some special style or design into his bookcase, it will be well to think over the various styles before deciding upon any particular one. Before going thoroughly into the working details a few preliminary words may be permitted.

Let the tools be always in keeping with the book, both in size and character. Large ones should be used only on a large book, and those of less size for smaller works. A book on Natural History should have a bird, insect, shell, or other tool indicative of the contents. A flower should be used on works on Botany, and all other works be treated in the same emblematical manner; so that the nature of the book may be understood by a glance at the back. In lettering, see that the letters are of a size proportionate to the book—legible, but not too bold. They should neither be so large as to prevent the whole of the title being read at one view, nor so small as to present a difficulty in ascertaining the subject of a book when on the shelf.

Amongst a large number of books there should be an agreeable variety of styles, so that the effect may be in harmony with the colours around, and produce as pleasing a contrast as possible.

Tools and Materials required for Finishing.—*Rolls, fillets, pallets,* centre and corner tools of every possible class and character; type of various sizes for the lettering of books

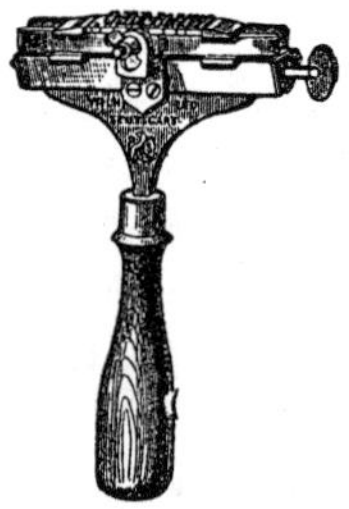

Type-holder.

Pallet.

Fillet.

or labels. The type may be either of brass or of the usual printer's metal; if the latter be chosen, care must be taken that it be not left at the fire too long, or it will melt. Type-holders to hold the type, which are made to fit the respective sizes are necessary, but one or two with a spring side, adjusted by screw at the side, will be found convenient for any sized type. In England it is the custom to letter books with *hand letters,* each letter being separate and fixed in a handle. I have, however, little doubt that these will in time be laid aside, and that the type and type case will be found in every bookbinder's shop.

Polishing irons. Of these two are necessary—one for the sides and one for the backs. There is generally a third kept for polishing the board end papers when pasted down, which should be kept for this purpose only.

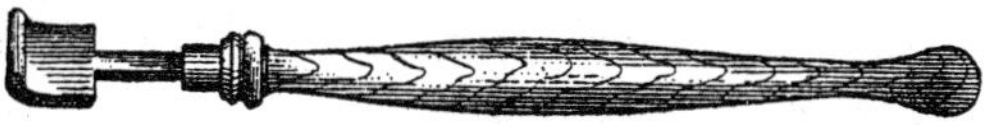

Polishing Iron.

A gold-rag, to wipe off the surplus gold from the back or side of a book. It should have a little oil well worked into it, so that when it has been wiped over the back or side the gold may adhere and remain in it. This rag when full of gold will be of a dirty yellow, and may then be melted down by any of the gold-refiners and the waste gold recovered.

India-rubber, cut up very small—the smaller the better—and steeped in turpentine, so as to render it as soft as possible, to be used for clearing away any gold not taken off by the gold-rag. This should also be melted down when full.[1]

Gold-cushion, for use as explained in Chapter XVII.

Gold leaf. The best should be used, it keeps its colour better, and is much more easy to work than the commoner metal usually sold.

Sponges, both large and small—the large ones for paste-washing, the smaller for glairing and sizing.

Glaire may be purchased already prepared, or it may be made from the white of egg, which must be very carefully beaten up to a froth with an egg whisk. In breaking the egg care must be taken not to let any of the yolk get amongst the white. A little vinegar should be mixed with the white before beating up, and a drop of ammonia, or a grain or two of common table salt, or a small piece of camphor, will in some measure prevent it from turning putrid,

[1] Messrs. Cow and Co., Cheapside, have lately prepared my rubber ready for use. I find it of great convenience.

as it is liable to do. Some workmen always have a stock of "good old glaire," as they term it, by them, fancying that it produces better work, but this is a mistaken notion, often productive of annoyance, and destructive to the comfort of the workmen. I advise the finisher to beat his glaire from an egg as he may require it. When well beaten, allow it to stand for some hours, and then pour the clear liquid into a bottle for use. I have had some dried albumen sent me, but its working has not given me such satisfaction as that freshly prepared; it may answer the purpose in other hands, but with me the gold appears to have been burnt in.

Cotton wool, for taking up the gold leaf and pressing it firmly on the leather.

Varnish should always be used on that part where glaire has been applied, after it has been polished; the object being to retain the brilliancy, and to preserve the leather from the ravages of flies and other insects which are attracted by the glaire; these pests do great damage to the covers of books which have been prepared with glaire, by eating it off. They also take away the surface of the leather and spoil the good appearance of the books. Varnish may be purchased at all prices: use only the best, and be very sparing with it.

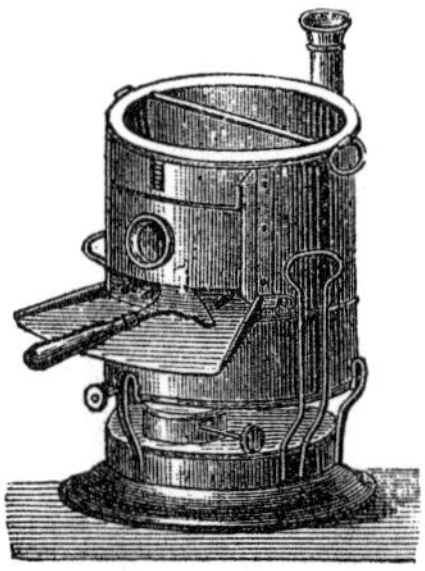

Leo's Oil Finishing Stove.

A small pair of spring *dividers*, some *lard*, *sweet oil*, and lastly, but most important, the *finishing stove*. Before gas was introduced the finishing stove in use was the now almost extinct charcoal fire. A bookbinder's gas stove can now be purchased at almost any gasfitter's shop or bookbinders' material dealers. The price varies according to size.

A stove burning paraffin oil may now be had from Leo of

Stuttgart, which he guarantees smokeless and free from soot; where gas is not obtainable, this will be found very handy.

Many still prefer the charcoal fire. To such a stove a pipe should be fixed to conduct the fumes away into the open air or up a chimney. To make such a stove any old tin may be utilized. Make a number of large holes through the sides; fill it with some live charcoal, and place a perforated tin plate on the top. It will keep alight for hours, and impart quite enough heat for any purpose required. This primitive stove, however, must be placed on a stand or on a piece of thick iron, lest it become dangerous. A *finishing press* is a small press, having two sides of

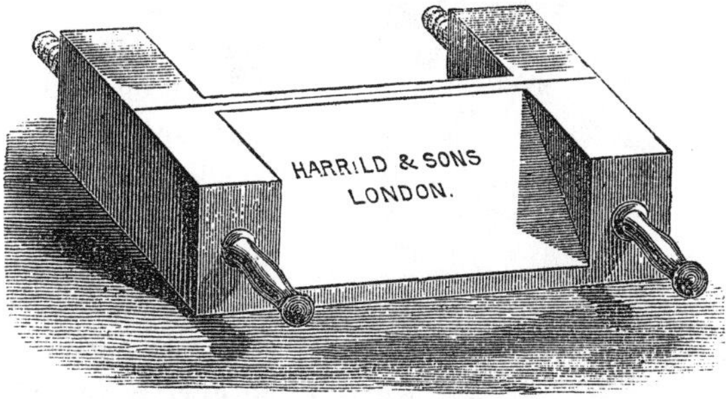

Finishing Press. The reverse side is quite flat, used when sides of books are being finished.

solid wood with wooden screws at each end, the cheeks should be of width enough to allow the sides of a book to be finished comfortably when the boards are extended, the book itself being held by the press which is screwed up tightly. The press should, however, be light enough to enable the finisher to easily turn it round, as it frequently must be, while finishing a book.

Mr. Leo has a press (patented) which he claims gives more freedom for finishing a book, but with it one can only finish the back of a book; there are, however, many good points that our English makers may well study.

Finishing is divided into two classes—*blind* or *antique*, or, as it is sometimes called, *monastic* and *gold-finished*.

The term antique is mostly known in the trade; and when *morocco antique* or *calf antique* is mentioned, it means that the whole of the finishing is to be done in blind tooling. Not only this, but that the boards should be very thick and bevelled, and the edges either dull gilt or red, or gilt over red. This class of work is used extensively for religious books. A gold line introduced and intermixed with blind work gives a great relief to any class of antique work.

Leo's Finishing Press.

It is not necessary that a special set of tools be kept for antique work, although some would look quite out of keeping if worked in gold. As a general rule antique tools are bold and solid, such as Venetian tools, whilst those for gold work are cut finer and are well shaded. The greater number work equally well in gold and in blind, but when a special style has to be followed the various tools and their adaptation to that style must be studied.

The general colour of the blind work is dark brown, and the proper way of working these antique tools is to take them warm and work them on the damp leather a number of times, thus singeing or burning as it were the surface only, until it has assumed its proper degree of colour.

Antique work, as a decoration, requires quite as much dexterity and care as gold work. Every line must be straight, and the tools must be worked properly on the leather, both in colour and depth; and as the tools have to be worked many times on the same spot, it requires a very steady hand and great care not to double them. Some consider blind work as preparatory to gold work, and that it gives experience in the method of handling and working the various tools, and the degree of heat required for different leathers without burning them through. The leather on which this work is mostly executed is morocco and calf.

In finishing the back of a book it must always be held

Antique Stamps.

tightly in the "finishing press." When in the press, mark the head and tail as a guide for the pallets by running a folding-stick along the edge of a piece of parchment or vellum held by the finger and thumb of the left hand against the sides of the volume across the back at the proper place. When two or more books of the same character and size are to range together, the backs must be compassed up so that the lines head and tail may run continuous when finished. In using the pallet, hold it firmly in the right hand, and let the working motion proceed from the wrist only, as if it were a pivot. It will be found rather difficult at first to work the pallets straight over the back and even to the sides of the bands, but after a little practice it will become easy to accomplish.

Morocco. Flexible work, as a rule, has blind lines, a broad and a narrow one, worked close to the bands. Damp the back with a sponge and clean water, and work the moisture evenly into the leather with a hard clean brush. Take a pallet of a size suitable to the book, warm it over the stove, and work it firmly over the back. As the leather dries, make the pallet hotter; this will generally be found sufficient to produce the required dark lines. Sometimes it will be necessary to damp the different places two or three times in order to get the proper colour in the blind tooling.

The tools may have a tendency to stick to the leather and possibly burn it. To obviate this, take 1¼ oz. of white wax and 1 oz. of deer fat or lard, place them in a pipkin over a fire or in a warm place, so that they may be well mixed together; when mixed allow them to cool. Rub some of this mixture upon the rough or fleshy side of a piece of waste morocco, and when working any tools in blind, rub them occasionally over the prepared surface. This mixture will be found of great service in getting the tools to *slip* or *come away* from the leather in working. Lard alone is sometimes used, but this mixture will be found of greater service to any finisher, and the advantage of adding the wax will be apparent.

The lines impressed on the back must now have their gloss given to them. This is done by *giggering* the pallets over them. Make the pallet rather hot, rub it over the greased piece of leather, and work it backwards and forwards in the impression previously made. Great care must be taken that the pallet be kept steadily in the impressions already made, or they will be doubled. The back is now ready for lettering. This will be found further on, classed under gold work.

To blind tool the side of a book it must be marked with a folder and straight edge, according to the pattern to be produced, and as a guide for the rolls and tools to be used. These lines form the ground plan for any design that has to be worked. Damp the whole of the side with a sponge, and brush it as before directed; then work the fillets along the lines marked. Run them over the same line two or three times. When dry, make the fillet immovable by driving a wooden wedge between the roll and fork, and gigger it backwards and forwards to produce the gloss. If tools are to be worked, make them slightly warm, and as the leather dries make the tool hotter and hotter. This must be repeated as often as is necessary, until the desired depth of colour and gloss is obtained. In using a roll that has a running or continuous pattern, a mark should be made upon the side with a file, at the exact point that first comes in contact with the leather, so that the same flower, scroll, or other design, may always fall in the same place in the repeated workings. It is impossible for a roll to be cut so exactly that it may be worked from any point in the circumference without doubling the design. All blind work is done in the same manner, whether in using a small or a large tool, *viz.*, the leather must be damped and repeatedly worked until the depth of colour is obtained. It is then allowed to dry, and re-worked to produce the gloss. The beauty of blind work consists in making the whole of the finishing of one uniform colour, in other words, avoiding the fault of having any portion of the work of lighter tint than the rest.

Gold Work is far more complicated than blind or antique work, so that it will be better if one practises upon some spare pieces of roan, calf, or morocco before one attempts to finish a book. Gold work is not more difficult than blind tooling, it is only more complicated. The different kinds of leather require such different degrees of heat, that what would fail to make the gold adhere upon one leather would burn through another. The various colours each require their different degrees of heat; as a rule, light fancy colours require less heat than dark ones. The finisher has not only to contend with these difficulties, but he must also become an adept in handling the gold leaf and in using the proper medium by which the gold is made to adhere to the leather. This medium is used in two ways—wet and dry. The wet is used for leather, the dry for velvet, satin, silk, and paper.

The wet medium is again divided into two classes, one for non-porous and another for porous leather. Morocco is the principal of the non-porous leathers, with roan and all other imitation morocco.

The porous varieties consist of calf of all kinds, russia, and sheep.

The non-porous leathers need only be washed with thin paste-water or vinegar, and glaired once; but if the glaire be thin or weak it will be necessary to give them a second coat.

The porous varieties must be paste-washed carefully, sized all over very evenly, and glaired once or twice; care being taken that the size and glaire be laid on as evenly as possible.

All this, although apparently so simple, must be well kept in mind, because the great difficulty that apprentices have to contend with is, that they do not know the proper medium for the various leathers, and one book may be prepared too much, while another may have a deficiency, and as a consequence, one book will be spoilt by the preparation cracking, and the gold not adhere to the other. By following the directions here given the finisher will find that his gold will adhere without much trouble, beyond the practice necessary in becoming accustomed to an accurate use of the various tools.

Suppose that a half morocco book is before us to be neatly finished and lettered. Take a broad and narrow pallet of a suitable and proper size, and work it against the bands in blind as a guide for finishing in gold. As the impression need be but very slight, warm the pallet on the gas stove but very little. Choose some suitable tool as a centre piece to go between the bands. Work this also lightly on the back exactly in the centre of each panel. This must be worked as truly as possible and perfectly straight. A line made previously with a folding-stick along the centre of the back will greatly assist in the working of a tool in its proper position. Now wash the back with vinegar, and brush it well with a hard brush to disperse the moisture and drive it equally into the leather; some use paste-water for this purpose instead of vinegar. Paste-water has a tendency to turn grey in the course of time, and this is avoided in using vinegar; vinegar also imparts freshness to the morocco, and keeps it moist a longer time, which is very desirable when finishing morocco.

The impressions made by the broad and narrow pallet and the centre tool are now to be pencilled in with glaire; when dry, pencil in another coat; allow this again to dry, then rub them very slightly with a piece of oiled cotton wool. Take a leaf of gold from the book and spread it out evenly on the gold cushion; cut it as nearly to the various shapes and sizes of the tools as possible. Now take up one of the pieces of gold upon a large pad of cotton wool, previously greased slightly by drawing it over the head. (There is always a sufficient amount of natural grease in the hair to cause the gold to adhere to the cotton when so treated.) Lay the gold gently but firmly on the impressed leather. See that the whole of the impression is covered, and that the gold is not broken. Should it be necessary to put on another piece of gold leaf, gently breathing on the first will make the second adhere. When all the impressions are covered with gold leaf, take one of the tools heated to such a degree that when a drop of water is applied it does *not hiss* but *dries* instantly; work it exactly in the blind impressions. Repeat this to the whole of the impressions, and wipe the overplus of gold off with the gold rag. The impressions are now supposed to be worked properly in gold; but if there are any parts where the gold does not adhere, they must be re-glaired and worked in again. A saucer should be placed near at hand, with water and a piece of rag or a sponge in it, to cool any tool and reduce it to its proper heat before using. If the tool be used too hot, the gold impression will be dull; if too cold, the gold will not adhere. To use all tools of the exact degree of heat required is one of the experiences of the skilled workman. The back is now ready for the title. Set up the proper words in a type-case, of a type sufficiently large and suitable to the book. The chief word of the title should be in somewhat larger size than the rest, the others diminishing, so that a pleasant arrangement of form be attained. In order to adjust the length of the words, it may be necessary to *space* some of them—that is, to put between each letter a small piece of metal called a *space*. Square the type, or make the face of the letters perfectly level, by pressing the face of them against a flat surface before tightening the screw. They must be exactly level one with another, or in the working some of them will be invisible. Screw up the type-case, warm it over the finishing stove, and work the letters carefully in blind as a guide. Damp the whole of the lettering space with vinegar. When dry, pencil the impressions in twice with glaire. Then lay the gold on and work them in gold.

But with lead type and a spring type-case (a method more suitable for some binders on account of its relative cheapness and the convenience of the case fitting itself to the different sizes of the type, of which the binder will want a selection of various sizes), the type-case must be warmed before the type is put in. The heat of the case should impart sufficient heat for the type to be worked properly. If the case and type be put on the stove, the type will probably be melted if not watched very narrowly. Hand letters are letters fixed in handles, each used as a single tool. The letters should be arranged in alphabetical order round the finishing stove, and as each letter is wanted it is taken from the order, worked, and replaced. They are still very much used in England, but where two or more books are to have the same lettering, brass type is very much better. It does its work more uniformly than hand letters, however skillfully used.

When this simple finishing can be executed properly and with ease, a more difficult task of finishing may be attempted, such as a *full gilt back.* This is done in two ways, a "run-up" back and a "mitred" back. As a general rule morocco is always mitred. Place the book on its side, lift up the mill-board, and make a mark head and tail on the back, a little away from the hinge of the back. Then with a folder and straight edge mark the whole length of the back: this is to be done on both sides. Make another line the whole length down the exact centre of the back. With a pair of dividers take the measurement of the spaces between the bands, and mark the size, head and tail, for the panels from the top and bottom band; with a folder and strip of parchment make a line across the back, head and tail, at the mark made by the dividers. Work a thin broad and narrow pallet alongside the bands in blind. Prepare the whole of the back with vinegar and glaire, as above described, but lay the glaire on with a sponge. When dry, lay the gold on, covering the whole of the back with it, mending any breaks. For mitreing, take a two-line pallet that has the ends cut at an angle of 45°, so that the joint at that angle may be perfect. Work this on the side at the

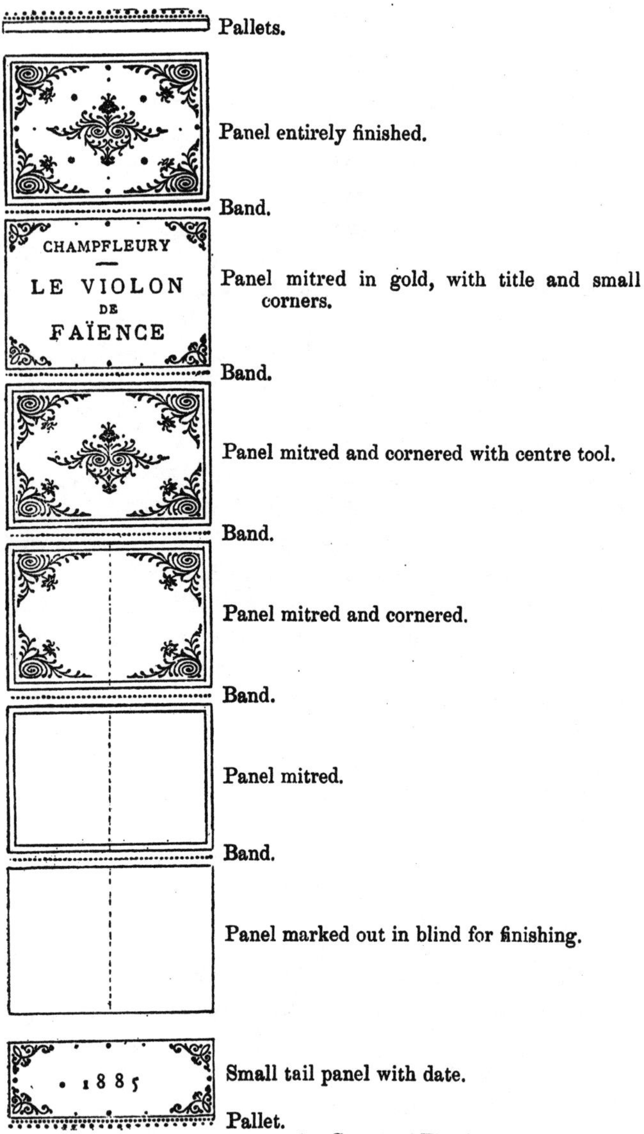

Showing progressive Stages of Finishing.

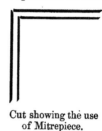

mark made up the back, and up to the line made in blind across the back. Repeat this to each panel. The two-line pallet must be worked across the back and up to the lines made in gold; the cutting of the pallet at the angle will allow of the union or mitre, so that each panel is independent of the other. There will be a space left, head and tail, which may be filled up with any fancy pallet or repetition of tools. The corners should be in keeping with the centre, and large enough to fit the panel. Work these from the sides of the square made, or from the centre of the panel, as will be found most convenient, according to the thickness of the book and style of finishing, and then fill in any small stops. When the whole is done, rub the gold off with the gold-rag, and use the india-rubber if necessary. The title has now to be put on, which is done in the same manner as before described.

Cut showing the use of Mitrepiece.

It is not always necessary that the finishing be done in blind first. I have explained it, and advocate its being so worked first as easier for a learner. One who is accustomed to finishing finds that a few lines marked previously with a folding-stick is all that is required. When working the title, a thread of silk drawn tightly across the gold produces a line sufficient, and is the only guide that an experienced workman requires.

To finish a side, make a mark with the folder and straight edge as a guide for any rolls or fillets. Prepare the leather as before described where the ornamentation is to come; but if the pattern is elaborate it must be worked first in blind. As a greater facility, take a piece of paper of good quality and well sized. Draw the pattern you wish to produce on the paper, and if any tools are to be used, hold them over the flame of gas; this will smoke them so that they may be worked on the paper in black. When the pattern is complete in every detail, tip the four corners of the paper with a little paste, then work the pattern through the paper on to the leather, using the various sized gouges as the scrolls require, and a single line fillet where there are lines. Work thus the complete pattern in blind. This being done completely, take the paper off from the four corners, place it on the other side, and work it in the same way. Prepare the leather with vinegar, and pencil out with glaire the whole of the pattern. If the whole side be glaired with a sponge it will leave a glossy appearance that is very undesirable. The whole of the side is now to be laid on with gold, and the pattern worked again with the warm tools, in the previous or blind impressions.

The inside of a book is generally finished before the outside. This should be done as neatly as possible, carefully mitreing the corners when any lines are used. Most frequently a roll is used, thus saving a great deal of time. A style was introduced in France called "doublé," the inside of the board being covered with a coloured morocco different to the outside, instead of having board papers. This inside leather was very elaborately finished; generally with a "dentelle" border, while the outside had only a line or two in blind. It is a style which, although very good in itself, is not now in great request, many prefer to have the finishing outside rather than to have it covered up and not seen when the book is shut.

The edges of the boards and the headbands must be finished either in gold or blind, according to fancy, but in keeping with the rest of the embellishment. A fine line worked on the centre of the edge of the board by means of a fillet looks better, and of course requires more pains than simply running a roll over it. If it is to be in gold, simply glairing the edge is sufficient. Lay on the gold and work the fillet carefully. Place the book on its ends in the

GROLIER.

Demy folio

finishing press to keep it steady, or it will shake and throw the fillet off. If a roll is used, take the gold up on the roll, but grease it first a little, by rubbing the gold rag over the edge to make the gold adhere. Then run the roll along the edge of the boards: the roll generally used for this purpose is called a *bar roll*—that is, one having a series of lines running at right angles with the edge of the roll.

Imitation morocco is generally used for publishers' bindings, where books are in large numbers and small in price, and the finishing is all done with the blocking press. To finish this leather by hand, it is advisable to wash it with paste-water and glaire twice.

Roan is generally used for circulating library work, and is very seldom finished with more than a few lines and the title across the back. This leather is prepared with paste-wash and glaire, and, when complete, varnished over the whole surface.

Inlaid Work.—Inlaid, or mosaic work, is used only in the higher branches of bookbinding. Formerly books were not inlaid, but painted with various colours. Grolier used a great deal of black, white, and green. Mr. Tuckett, the late binder to the British Museum, took out a patent for extracting one colour from leather and substituting another by chemical action. This method, however, was in use and known long before he turned his attention to the subject, although he improved greatly upon the old practice. As the patent has long expired, it may not be out of place to give an extract from the specification: "Take dark chocolate colour, and after the design has been traced thereon, it is then to be picked out or pencilled in with suitable chemicals, say diluted nitric acid; this will change the chocolate, leaving the design a bright red on a chocolate ground." But to lay on the various colours with leather is, no doubt, by far the better plan. Paint has a tendency in time to crack, and, if acids are used, they will, to a certain extent, rot or destroy the leather; but if leather is used it will always retain both colour and texture. To choose the proper colours that will harmonize with the ground, give tone, and produce a pleasing effect, requires a certain amount of study. Morocco is the leather generally used, but in Vienna calf has been used with very good results. If the pattern to be inlaid be very small, steel punches of the exact shape of the tools are used to punch or cut out the patterns required. To do this, work the pattern in blind on the side of the book; take morocco of a different colour to the ground it is required to decorate, and pare it down as thin as possible. Lay it on a slab of lead. Lead is better than anything else on account of its softness; the marks made by the punch can always be beaten out again, and when quite used up it may be re-melted and run out anew. Now take the steel punch of an exact facsimile of the tool used that is to be inlaid, and punch out from the leather the required number. These are to be pasted and laid very carefully on the exact spot made by the blind-tooling; press each down well into the leather, either with a folding-stick or the fingers, so that it adheres properly. When dry, the book should be pressed between polished plates, in order that the pieces that have been laid on, may be pressed well into the ground leather. When it has been pressed, the whole of the leather must be prepared as for morocco, and finished in gold. The tools in the working will hide all the edges of the various inlaid pieces, provided they are laid on exactly.

If interlacing bands are to be of various colours, the bands must be cut out. Pare the leather thin, and after working the pattern through the paper on to the sides of the book, lay it on the thinly pared leather; with a very sharp and pointed knife cut through the paper and leather together on a soft board. Or the design may be worked or drawn on a thin board, and the various bands cut out

MAIOLI.

Royal folio

of the board as patterns. Lay these on the thin leather and cut round them. Keep these board templates for any future use of the same patterns. The various pieces are to be well pasted, carefully adjusted in their places, and well rubbed down. The leather is then to be prepared and worked off in gold.

Another method is to work the pattern in blind on the sides. Pare the morocco thin, and while damp place it upon the portion of the pattern to be inlaid, and press it well with the fingers, so that the design is impressed into it. Lay the leather carefully on some soft board, and cut round the lines made visible by the pressure with a very sharp knife. When cut out, paste and lay them on the book and prepare as before, and finish in gold. I do not recommend this last method as being of much value; I give it only because it is sometimes chosen; but for any good work, where accuracy is required, either of the plans mentioned previously are to be preferred.

The Viennese work their calf in quite a different manner, in fact, in the same way that the cabinet-makers inlay their woodwork. With a very sharp and thin knife they cut right through two leathers laid the one on the other. The bottom one is then lifted out and replaced by the top one. By this method the one fits exactly into the other, so that, if properly done, the junctions are so neatly made that no finishing is required to cover the line where the two colours meet.

The frontispiece to this treatise is a copy of a book bound by my father for one of the Exhibitions. The ground is of red morocco, inlaid with green, brown, and black morocco. The pattern may be called "Renaissance." The inside of the boards are "Grolier," inlaid as elaborately as the outside. Seven months' labour was expended on the outside decoration of this volume.

Porous.—*Calf*, as before described, requires more and

different preparation than morocco, on account of its soft and absorbing nature. As a foundation or groundwork, paste of different degrees of strength is used, according to the various work required.

Calf books have generally a morocco lettering piece of a different colour to the calf on the back for the title. This is, however, optional, and may or may not be used, according to taste. Leather lettering pieces have a great tendency to peel off, especially if the book be exposed to a hot atmosphere, or if the paste has been badly made, so that it is perhaps better if the calf itself be lettered. There is no doubt that a better effect is produced in a bookcase when a good assortment of coloured lettering pieces are placed on the variously coloured backs, and the titles can be more easily read than if they were upon light or sprinkled calf; but where wear and tear have to be studied, as in public libraries, a volume should not have any lettering pieces. All such books should be lettered on their natural ground.

For lettering pieces, take morocco[1] of any colour, according to fancy, and having wetted it to facilitate the work, pare it down as thin and as evenly as possible. Cut it to size of the panel or space it is intended to fit. When cut truly, pare the edges all round, paste it well, put it on the place and rub well down. Should the book require two pieces—or one for the title, and one for the volume or contents—it is better to vary the colours. I must caution the workman not to allow the leather to come over on to the joint, as by the frequent opening or moving of the boards the edge of the leather will become loose. A very good plan as a substitute for lettering pieces is to colour the calf either dark brown or black, thus saving the leather at the expense of a little more time. When the lettering

[1] Other leathers are often used instead of morocco, even paper; in fact a specially prepared paper is largely sold in Germany for this purpose.

pieces are dry, mark the back, head and tail, for the pallets or other tools with a folding-stick. Apply with a brush paste all over the back. With a thick folding-stick, or with the handle of an old tooth brush, which is better, rub the paste into the back. Before it has time to dry, take the overplus off with rather a hard sponge, dipped in thin paste-water. The learner will perhaps wonder why paste of full strength should be used for the back, and only paste-water for the sides. The reason is, that through the stretching of the leather over the back in covering, the pores are more open, and consequently require more filling up to make a firm ground. Much depends upon the groundwork being properly applied; and a general caution with regard to the working in general may not be here amiss. Finishing, above all other departments, demands perfect cleanliness. A book may have the most graceful designs, the tools be worked perfectly and clearly, but be spoiled by having a dirty appearance. See that everything is clean—paste-water, size, glaire, sponges, and brushes. Do not lay any gold on until the preparation be perfectly dry, or the gold will adhere and cause a dirty yellow stain where wiped off.

Should the calf book be intended to have only a pallet alongside the bands, it is only necessary, when the paste-wash is quite dry, to glaire that portion which is to be gilt: this is usually done with a camel's hair brush, by laying on two coats. When dry, cut the gold into strips, and take one up on the pallet and work it on the calf. This is what is termed calf neat. The band on each side is gilt, leaving the rest of the leather in its natural state. Some binders polish their backs instead of leaving them dead or dull. This, however, is entirely according to taste, whether so large a space be left polished only.

Full Gilt Back.—Run-up. Make a mark up the back on both sides a little away from the joint with a folder and

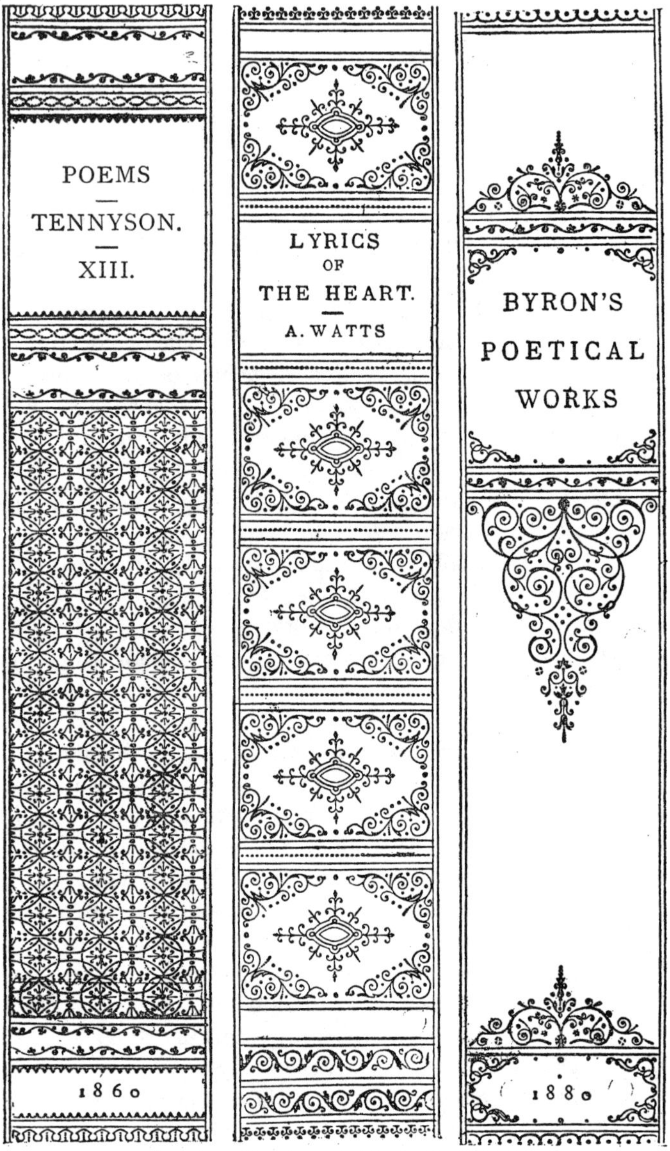

Samples of Backs suitable for Calf Work.

straight edge. Put on lettering piece. When dry, paste and paste-wash the back. When again dry, take some of Young's patent size, melt it in a pipkin with a little water and apply it with a sponge. Lay this on very evenly with a very soft sponge, and be particular that it is perfectly clean, so that no stains be left. When the size is done with, put it on one side for future use. This size should not be taken its full strength, and when warmed again some more water should be added to make up for evaporation. When the coat of size has dried, apply two coats of glaire. The first must be dry before the second is applied, and great care must be taken that the sponge is not passed over the same place twice, or the previous preparation will be taken off. It is now ready for finishing. Cut the gold to proper size; rub a little lard over the whole of the back with a little cotton wool. This requires great attention. Very little must be put on light or green calf, as these colours are stained very readily. Take the gold up on a cotton pad; lay it carefully down on the back; breathe on the gold, and press down again. If there be any places where the gold is broken, they must be mended. Now take a two-line fillet; heat it so that it hisses when placed in the cooling pan or the saucer with the wet rag in it, and run it the whole length of the back on the line made before paste-washing. Do this on both sides, and rub the gold off with the gold-rag up to the line on the outside. Take a two-line pallet, and work it on each side of the bands. Work the morocco lettering piece last, as it requires less heat. The centre piece of each panel must now be worked. Impress the tools firmly but quickly. The corner tools next; work them from the centre or sides, using the right hand corners as a guide, and judging the distance by the left ones. The press must be turned when it is required to bring the left side to the right hand in working the corners. The requisite pallets may now be worked to finish the book head and tail. As a rule these are worked when the two-line pallet is imprinted.

Calf requires very quick working. The tools should not be held over the various places too long, or the heat will destroy the adherent properties of the albumen. With morocco time does not signify so much, as the heat used is not so great.

Mitred back must be prepared the same way as for "run-up back," and the mitreing is to be done as explained in working morocco. As before stated, this is superior work and requires more skill; takes longer, but looks much better: each panel should be an exact facsimile of the rest. If the tools do not occupy precisely similar places in each panel, the result will be very unsatisfactory, and an evidence of a want of skill. When the backs are finished, rub the gold off with the gold-rag, and clear off any residue with the india-rubber. Be very careful that every particle of the surplus gold be cleaned off, or the delicate lines of the ornaments will be obscure and ragged in appearance.

The book is now ready for lettering. Set the type up in the case, and work it carefully in a perfectly straight line over the back. The whole of the back is now to be polished with the polishing iron, which must be perfectly clean and bright before it is used. Prepare a board from an old calf binding, by rubbing some fine emery or charcoal and lard over the leather side of it. By rubbing the iron over this prepared surface it will acquire a bright polish. It must be used over the back by holding it lightly, and giving it an oblong circular motion. Go over every portion of the back with very even pressure, so that no part may be made more glossy than another. The polishing iron should be used rather warmer than the tools. If the iron be too hot the glaire will turn white; if too cold the polish will be dull. The grease upon the leather will be quite sufficient to make the polisher glide easily over the surface, but the operation must be rapidly and evenly done. All light and green calf require less heat than any other kinds. These will turn black if the iron be in the least degree too hot.

It is in finishing the sides that the workman can show his good taste and skill. The sides should be always in keeping with the back; or, more strictly speaking, the back should be in keeping with the sides. Before the sides can be finished, the inside of the boards must occupy our attention. With a "run-up" back, the edge of the leather round the end papers is to be worked either in blind or have a roll round it in gold. In any case it should be paste-washed. If for blind, the roll is to be heated and worked round it; if for gold, it must be glaired twice. The gold, cut into strips, is to be taken up on the roll and worked, and the overplus taken off with the gold-rag as before directed. Extra work, such as mitred work, should have some lines, or other neat design impressed. Paste-wash the leather, and when dry glaire twice. When again dry lay on the gold all round, and work the roll or other fillets, or such other tool that may be in keeping with the exterior work. When the gold has been wiped off, the leather should be polished with the polishing iron.

The outside must now be finished. Are the sides to be polished, or left plain? If they are not to be polished, paste-wash the whole of the side up to the edge of the back carefully, then glaire only that portion which is to be gilt. Generally a two-line fillet only is used round the edge, so that the width of the fillet or roll must determine the width to be glaired. When glaired twice and dry, take up the gold on the fillet or roll and work it evenly and straightly round the edge. The corners where the lines meet are next to be stopped by working a small rosette or small star on them. Clean off any gold that may be on the side, and work a small dotted or pin-head roll at the edge of the glaire. This will cover and conceal the edge.

Extra calf books generally have the sides polished. Paste-wash the sides all over, and when dry size them. Hold the book, if small, in the left hand, if large, lay it on the press and work the sponge over the side in a circular direction, so that the size may be laid on as evenly as possible. Be very careful that it does not froth; should it do so, squeeze the sponge out as dry as possible, and fill it anew with fresh size. Some workmen work the sponge up and down the book, but if this be not done very evenly it produces streaks. The finisher will find he can lay a more even coating on by using the sponge in a circular direction. Allow this to dry by leaving the book with boards extended. When perfectly dry glaire once. This will be found sufficient, as the size gives body to the glaire. When sizeing and glairing, be assured that the book be laid down with the boards extended on a level surface; if the book be not level, the size or glaire will run down to the lowest portion of the surface, and become unequally distributed. The gold is now to be laid on the respective places, either broad or narrow, according to the nature of the finishing or width of the rolls. As a general rule, the sides of the better class of calf books have nothing more than a three-line round the edge and mitred in the corners. This is, however, quite a matter of taste. Some have a border of fancy rolls, but never any elaborate pattern as in morocco work. To finish the sides, place the book in the finishing press with the boards extended, so that they may rest on the press. This will afford greater facility for working the fillets, rolls, and tools necessary to complete the design on each side. The finishing press being a small one, can be easily turned round as each edge of the border is finished.

To polish the sides, place the book on its side on some

soft surface, such as a board covered with baize, and kept for the purpose. Use the large and heavy polishing iron, hot and clean. Rub or work the iron quickly and firmly over the sides, first from the groove towards the foredge, and then in a contrary direction, from the tail to the head, by turning the volume. The oil or grease applied to the cover previous to laying on the gold will be sufficient to allow the polisher to glide easily over the surface. Polishing has also the effect of smoothing down the burr formed on the leather by the gilding tools, and bringing the impressions slightly to the surface. The iron must be held very evenly, so that the centre of the iron may be the working portion. If held sideways the edge of the iron will indent the leather. The heat must be sufficient to give a polish. It must be remembered that if the iron is too hot it will cause the glaire to turn white. The temperature must be well tested before it be applied to the cover. A practised finisher can generally tell the proper heat on holding the iron at some little distance from his face, by the heat radiated from the iron. Calf books should be pressed, whether polished or not.

Pressing.—Plates of japanned tin or polished horn are proper for this purpose. Put pressing tins between the book and the mill-boards: the tins must be up to the joint. Now place one of the japanned plates on the side level with the groove; turn book and japanned plate over carefully together, so that neither shifts; place another of the polished plates on the top of the book, thus placing the book between two polished surfaces. Put the book into the standing press, and screw down tightly. Leave in for some hours. When pressed sufficiently, take the book out, and if the sides be polished, varnish them.

Make a little pad of cotton wool, saturate the lower portion with varnish; rub it on a piece of waste paper to equalize the varnish, then work the pad over the side as quickly as possible in a circular direction. Renew the wool with varnish for the other side. Enough must be taken on the pad to varnish the whole side, or the delay caused by renewing the varnish on the cotton will cause a streaked surface. When the varnish is perfectly dry—a few minutes will suffice—the book must be again pressed. To do this, rub the gold-rag, which is greased, over the sides, this will prevent the sides from sticking to the polished plates. Place the book between the plates as before, leaving out the pressing tins, and place in the standing press. Only little pressure must now be given; if the press be screwed down too tightly the plates will stick to the book. The varnish must be of good quality, and perfectly dry, or the result will be the same. Half an hour in the press will be found quite long enough. Should the plates stick, there is no other remedy than washing off the varnish with spirits of wine, and the glaire and size with warm water, and carefully re-preparing the surface as before. This is, however, an accident that cannot happen if due care and judgment be exercised.

Graining.—Graining is now used very much on calf books. It may be properly considered as a blind ornament. It is done by means of wooden, or, better still, copper plates cut out in various patterns, so as to form small squares, scales of fish, or an imitation of morocco. Place the volume between two of these plates, level to the groove of the back, in the standing press; screw down tightly. The pressure should be equal over the whole surface. Nothing looks worse than a bold impression in one place and a slight one in another, so that it is rather important that it be evenly pressed; a second application of the plates is impracticable. Graining has the advantage of hiding any finger-marks that may accidentally be on the calf, and also partly conceals any imperfections in the leather.

The state of the weather must in a great measure guide the finisher as to the proper number of volumes he ought to prepare at one time. The leather should always be a little moist, or, in other words, rather *fresh.* In winter double the number of books may be prepared, and the gold laid on, than the dryness of a summer's day will permit. If books are laid on over night the tools must be used very hot in working them the next morning, or the gold will not adhere. During summer, flies will eat the glaire from various places while the book is lying or standing out to dry, so that constant vigilance must be kept to avoid these pests.

Russia is prepared in the same way as calf, but is usually worked with more blind tools than gold, and the sides are not as a rule polished, so that the size and glaire are dispensed with, except on those parts where it is to be finished in gold; those portions need be only paste-washed and glaired once, without any size.

Finishing with Dry Preparation.—The dry preparation is used for silk, velvet, paper, or any other material that would be stained by the employment of the wet process. There are a number of receipts in the trade and in use.

Take the white of eggs, and dry by spreading it somewhat thickly over glass plates, taking care to preserve it from dust. When dry it will chip off readily, if the glass has been previously *very slightly* oiled or greased. It must not be exposed to more heat than 40° Reaum., or the quality of the albumen will be destroyed. The dried mass is to be well powdered in a porcelain mortar.

Or, take equal portions of gum mastic, gum sandrac, gum arabic, and powder them well in a mortar. This powder, if good work be desired, must be ground into an impalpable powder. When powdered put it into a box or bottle, and tie three or four thicknesses of fine muslin over the mouth. By tapping the inverted box, or shaking it over the lines or letters, the dust will fall through in a fine shower. The powder should fall only on the part to be gilt. Cut the gold into strips, take it up upon the tool, and work rather hot. The overplus of the powder can be brushed away when the finishing is completed. Finishing powder is now sold commercially.

Velvet is very seldom finished beyond having the title put on, and this should be worked in blind first and with moderately large letters, or the pile will hide them.

Silk is finished more easily, and can, if care be taken, have rather elaborate work put upon it. In such a case, the lines or tools, which must be blinded-in first, may be glaired. For this purpose the glaire must be put in a saucer or plate in the free air for a day or two, so that a certain amount of water or moisture of the glaire may be evaporated; but it must not be too stiff so as to prevent the brush going freely over the stuff. Great care, however, must be taken, or the glaire will spread and cause a stain. A thin coat of paste-water will give silk a body and keep the glaire from spreading to a certain extent, but I think the best medium for silk is the dry one, and it is always ready for instant use. In using glaire the gold is laid on the silk, but on no account must any oil or lard be rubbed on it for the temporary holding of the gold. Rub the parts intended for the gold with the finger (passed through the hair), or with a clean rag lightly oiled, and when the tools are re-impressed a clean piece of flannel should be used to wipe off the superfluous gold.

Blocking has been used lately on silk with some success in Germany. The blocking plate is taken out of the press, and the gold is laid on it, and then replaced in the press. The finishing powder is freely distributed over the silk side, which is laid on the bed of the press. On pulling the lever over, the block descends and imprints the design in gold on the silk. This process may be applied to velvet, but velvet never takes the sharpness of the design on account of the pile, so that as a rule it is left in its natural state.

Vellum.—The Dutch, as a nation, appear to have been the first to bind books in vellum. It was then a simple kind of casing, with hollow backs. A later improvement of theirs was that of sewing the book on double raised cords, and making the book with a tight back, similar to the way in which our flexible books are now done, showing the raised bands. The ornamentation was entirely in blind, both on the back and sides, and the tools used were of a very solid character.

This art of binding in vellum seems to be entirely lost at the present day; its imperishable nature is indeed its only recommendation. It has little beauty; is exceedingly harsh; and little variety can be produced even in the finishing.

There are two or three kinds of vellum prepared from calf skins at the present day, thanks to the progress of invention. First, we have the prepared or artist's vellum, with a very white artificial surface; then the Oxford vellum, the surface of which is left in its natural state; the Roman vellum, which has a darker appearance. Parchment is an inferior animal membrane prepared from sheepskins after the manner of vellum, and this is very successfully imitated by vegetable parchment, made by immersing unsized paper for a few seconds in a bath of diluted oil of vitriol. This preparation resembles the animal parchment so closely that it is not easy to distinguish the difference. It is used very extensively in France for wrappering the better class of literature, instead of issuing them in cloth as is the custom here.

The method of finishing vellum is altogether different to leather. On account of its very hard and compact nature, it requires no other ground or preparation than glaire for gold work.

The cover should be very carefully washed with a soft sponge and clean water, to clean off any dirt or finger-marks, and to make the book look as fresh as possible. This washing must be very carefully done by going over the surface as few times as possible. This caution applies particularly to the prepared or artist vellum, as each washing will take off a certain amount of the surface, so that the more it is damped and rubbed the more the surface will be disturbed and the beauty destroyed. It requires some experience to distinguish the flesh and leather surfaces of prepared vellum, but this experience must be acquired, because it is absolutely necessary that the leather side should be outward when the book is covered, for two reasons: the flesh side is more fibrous, and adheres better to the boards than the leather side, and the leather side is less liable to have its surface disturbed in the process of washing.

The parts that are to be gilt must be glaired, but as the glaire will show its presence, or, more strictly speaking, leave rather a dirty mark, the tools should first be worked in blind, and the glaire laid on carefully up to their outer edge. When dry, lay the gold on and work the tool in. Let the tools be only moderately warm; if too hot they will go through to the mill-board, leaving their mark as if they had been cut out with a knife.

As a rule no very heavy tooling is ever put on vellum, the beauty lies in keeping the vellum as clean as possible. The tooling being, comparatively speaking, on the surface, owing to the thinness of the skin, requires a very competent and clean workman to produce anything like good work on vellum.

Vellum is of so greasy a nature that, if a title-piece of leather has to be put on, it will be found that there is a great difficulty in making it adhere properly unless some special precaution be taken. The best plan is to scrape the surface where the leather is intended to be placed with the edge of a knife. This will produce a rough and fibrous ground on which to place the pasted leather. This *leather*, when dry, must be prepared with paste-water and glaire, in the same manner as with other books.

In the foregoing instructions for finishing a book, the most that can be looked for towards teaching either the apprentice or the unskilled workman is to give him an idea how it is accomplished by practised hands. Pure taste, a correct eye, and a steady hand, are not given to all in common. The most minute instructions, detail by detail, cannot make a workman if Nature has denied these gifts. I have known men whose skill in working a design could not be excelled, but who could not be trusted to gild a back without instructions. Others, whose ideas of design were not contemptible, could not tool two panels of a back in perfect uniformity. Some also have so little idea of harmony of colour, that without strict supervision they would give every volume the coat of a harlequin. In a word, a first-rate bookbinder is *nascitur non fit*, and although the hints and instructions I have penned may not be sufficient to *make* a workman, I trust they will be found of some value to the skilled as well as to the less practised craftsman.

Blocking.—The growing demand for books that were at once cheap and pretty, became so strong, that mechanical appliances were invented to facilitate their ornamentation; and thus we have the introduction of the present blocking press.

I will not follow too closely the various improvements introduced at different periods, but roughly describe the blocking press, without which cheap bookbinding cannot be done at the present day. There can be no doubt that this press owes its extensive use to the introduction of publishers' cloth work.

Formerly, when the covers of books were blocked, a

small lying or other press was used. The block, previously heated, was placed on the book, and the screw or screws turned to get a sufficient pressure. It often happened that the pressure was either too much or too little: the block either by the one accident sank into the leather too deeply, or by the other the gold failed to adhere, and it required a good workman to work a block properly.

The first press to be noticed is a Balancier, having a moveable bed, a heating box, heated by means of red-hot irons, two side pillars to guide the box in a true line, and attached to it a screw connected at the top with a bar or arm, having at each extremity an iron ball. The block, having been fixed to a plate at the bottom of the heated box, the side of the book was laid down on the bed, and by swinging the arm round the block descended upon the book. The arm was then swung back, and the next book put into place. It will be seen that this incurred a great loss of time.

The next improvement consisted in having a press that only moved a quarter circle, with almost instantaneous action; and another improvement connected with the bed was, that by means of screws and gauges, when the block was once set, a boy or an inexperienced hand might with ease finish off hundreds of copies, all with equal pressure. By referring to the woodcut opposite, the press and its action will be seen and understood. The box may be heated with gas, and kept at a constant and regulated temperature the whole time of working. It can be adjusted to any amount of pressure, as it is regulated by the bed underneath.

The next step in progress was the introduction of printing in different colours upon the cloth, and intermixing them with gold. Messrs. Hopkinson and Cope's machines may be mentioned. They are made to be driven by steam, and will print and emboss from 500 to 600 covers per hour, and are heated by steam or gas. The inking apparatus is placed at the back of the press, so that while the workman is placing another cover, the ink roller, by automatic action, inks the block ready for the next impression. The inking or printing of the covers is done without heat, so, to avoid loss of time, an arrangement is made that the heating box can be cooled immediately by a stream of water passed through it.

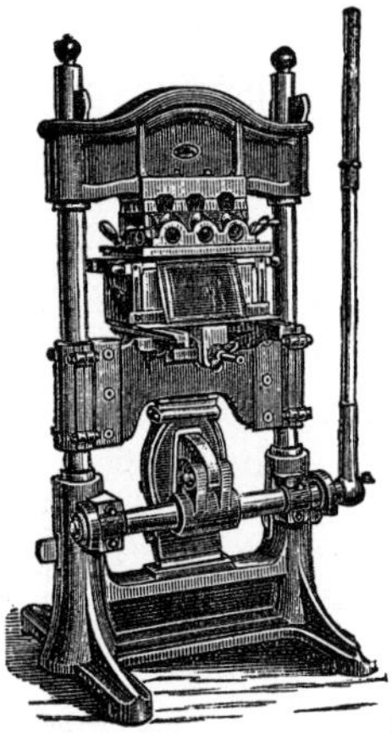

Messrs. Kampe and Co. have just brought out a blocking machine, which they claim to be superior to any in the trade. It will block at the rate of 700 to 800 covers per hour. The pressure is obtained by one of the most powerful of mechanical appliances, and it can be adjusted to block either paper or leather.

The tools required for blocking are called blocks or stamps. These may be composed of very small pieces, or may be of one block cut to the size of the book. In any case, the block has to be fastened to the moveable plate at the bottom of the heating box. To block the sides of a book, take a stout piece of paper and glue it upon a moveable plate.[1] Then take the book, and having set the blocks upon the side in exact position, place the side or board upon which are placed the blocks upon the bed of the blocking press, leaving the volume hanging down in front of the press. The bed is now to be fixed, so that the centre of the board is exactly under and in the centre of the heating box. When quite true, the sides and back gauges are fixed by screws. Pull the lever so that a slight pressure upon the plate be given: release

[1] The moveable plate is also called the *platen.*

the press, and take out the book and examine if all be correct. Some of the blocks may require a small piece of paper as a pad, so as to increase the pressure, others to be shifted a little. Now glue the back of the stamps and replace them in their respective places. Place the whole under the top plate in the press, heat the box, and pull the lever over; and let the book remain for some little time to set the glue. Take out the book, examine if perfectly square and correct, but replace it with a soft mill-board under the stamps, and pull down the press. The lever must remain over, and the blocks be under pressure until the glue is hardened.

Another method is to glue upon the plate a piece of thick paper and mark upon it the exact size of the book to be blocked. Strike upon the plate from the size the centre, and from that any other lines that may assist in placing the blocks. Arrange the blocks upon the plate so as to form the design; when correct, paste the blocks on their backs and replace them on the plate. When the paste adheres a little, turn the plate over and put it into the press. Apply heat to the box; pull the lever over, and when the paste is set, regulate the bed and gauges.

When the press is properly heated, throw back the lever; take out the mill-board from under the stamp, and regulate the degree of pressure required by the side-screw under or over the bed. Place upon the bed the side to be stamped, hold it firmly against the guides with the left hand, and with the right draw the lever quickly to the front. This straightens the toggels and forces down the heating box, causing a sharp impression of the stamp upon the leather or other material. Throw or let the lever go back sharply, and take out the book. If the block be of such a design that it must not be inverted, the whole of the covers must be blocked on one side first, and the block turned round for the other side, or the design will be upside down.

Work for blocking in gold does not require so much body or preparation as if it were gilt by hand. Morocco can be worked by merely washing the whole surface with a little urine or weak ammonia, but it is safer to use a coat of glaire and water mixed in proportion of one of the former to three of the latter. The heat should not be great, and slowly worked.

Calf should have a coat of milk and water or thin paste-water as a ground, and when dry another of glaire. Both should be laid on as evenly as possible; but if only portions are to be gilt, such as a centre-piece, and the rest dead, the centre-piece or other design should be pencilled in with great care. The design should be first slightly blocked in blind as a guide for the glairing. The edge of the glaire generally leaves a black or dark stain. The heat required for calf is greater than for morocco, and the working must be done more quickly.

Cloth requires no preparation whatever, the glue beneath and the coloured matter on the cloth gives quite enough adhesiveness when the hot plate comes down for the gold to adhere.

A great deal of taste may be displayed in the formation of patterns in this branch, but as publishers find that books that are tawdrily gilt are better liked by the public, they are, of course, very well satisfied if their books are well covered with gold. It would be well if those who have the principal charge of this work would strive, by the cultivation of elegant design, to correct the vitiated taste of the public, and seek by a study of classic ornamentation to please the eye and satisfy the judgment rather than to attract the vulgar by glitter and gaudy decoration.

However, of late years a great advancement has been made with publishers' block work; the samples given in the trade paper ("The Bookbinder" now "Bookmaker") will prove this.

GENERAL INFORMATION.

CHAPTER XXIV.

WASHING AND CLEANING.

THE binder is often called upon to clean books; to many he is a sort of Aladdin, who makes old books into new; the consequence is that he often has placed in his hands a lot of dirty, miserable-looking books, and is expected to turn them into first-class copies. To renovate such books requires time and experience, and unfortunately very little is known among binders as a body about cleaning. Outside the trade, I am sorry to say, even less is known, for if a book be received from a binder bleached, it seems to satisfy the owner, and to be all that is desired. By such treatment of bleaching a quantity of lime is generally left in the paper, the goodness is destroyed, and naturally the paper must suffer in a short time. To test such treatment one has only to apply the tongue to the paper, it will at once absorb any moisture, as blotting paper does, and often the lime can be distinctly tasted.

But books are often washed and given out to the binder to rebind in this state. In such a case it remains with the binder not to associate himself with the book; for if he rebinds such a book the stigma will attach itself to him when the period of rotting, falling to pieces, and other misfortunes has arrived.

It is the practice of many who profess to wash books or prints to use chlorine at every washing; this is not necessary; often a simple bath of hot water, with perhaps the addition of a little alum, is all that is required. An important thing is to know the different kinds of stains when looking through the book; there may be many in one book, each from a different cause. In such a case it will be best to go for the majority, and to use the bath that will move them. Often the one bath is sufficient, but should there be any stains that are not touched, these leaves must be treated again.

When there are stains of different character in the one book, such as oil stains on a few leaves, and, say, coffee stains in other parts, the oil must be first removed; the one bath will not touch both stains.

Often when the bath is used wrongly it will fix the stain in the paper, and not remove it, the chemical used acting as a mordant.

It is impossible for me to describe the various stains, the intelligence of the workman must be brought to bear on the subject; and I advise a small memo. book be used to jot down the difficulties that may occur from time to time, and so to act as a guide for future work; to the use of such a book I am enabled to lay before my readers the methods of working with the various receipts collected in France and Germany, and used by me in my business.

To wash a book it is absolutely necessary to pull it to pieces. Should there be much glue on the back, and difficulty arise in the pulling, the book may be treated as given in Chapter II.: or sections of six or eight sheets may be left together; the hot water and soaking to which the book will be subjected in the washing will dissolve the glue or paste that may be on the back, and the sheets will readily part whilst in the solution. Washing must be conducted with great care; the handling of the wet sheets will demand the most delicate touch, for one can reasonably understand that paper left in water for twelve or more hours is likely to be very tender. In nearly every case when a book has been washed it will be found necessary to size it: the size gives back the body or goodness that the hot water and chemical has extracted. Often the virtue is extracted by damp, through the book being left in some damp situation, or by imperfect sizing the paper has first received; in such cases, although the book may not require washing, sizing will be of benefit.

Requisites.—The necessary articles required for washing, etc., are dishes. Those of porcelain are perhaps the best; they may be bought at any photographic material dealers. If much work is done, it is advantageous to have a set or sets of two or three sizes. In using the various dishes, ample room should be given to allow the hands to enter the water and pick up the sheets or leaves without any danger of tearing. Should the pans be of such a size as to be too heavy to move when full of water, they may be emptied by means of a syphon, the short end of the syphon placed, in preference, at one of the corners of the dish, so as not to touch the sheets. The dishes may also be made of wood, lined with zinc or lead: for very large work these must be used, the porcelain are not made above a certain size.

A *kettle* for boiling water in.

A *gas-stove*, or substitute, for heating purposes.

A *peel*, made of wood, to hang the sheets on the lines. The sheets are placed on the peel, from which they are transferred to the lines.

Chloride of lime for solution of chloride of lime.—Make a saturated solution of chloride of lime by mixing intimately the lime with water in a large jar. When clear the solution may be used. To every gallon of hot water take from this stock solution two or three ounces.

NOTE.—*Chlorine bleaches all vegetable matter.*

Hydrochloric acid, also known as muriatic acid or spirits of salts (poison)

Oxalic acid (poison).

Powdered alum.

A *hair sieve.* This is not absolutely necessary, as a fine piece of linen will answer as well.

Size :—

(1). 1 quart of water.
½ ounce of powdered alum.
1 ounce of isinglass.
1 scruple of soap.

Simmer the whole for about one hour, then pass through a fine hair sieve or piece of linen. Use this whilst warm.

(2.) 1 gallon of water.
½ lb. of best glue.
2 ounces of powdered alum.

Simmer and use as above.

(3). 1 quart of water.
2½ ounces of isinglass.
2 drachms of alum.

Simmer the whole for about one hour, strain as above.

It must be remembered that a size too strong in glue or isinglass is liable to make the paper too brittle; again, some papers require a stronger size than others.

(4). A size that may be used cold, and is recommended in France, to keep at hand and to use when only a single leaf requires sizing, such as when a name has been erased from a title-page, is as follows:—Boil about a quart of water in a saucepan. Whilst boiling, add about two oz. of shellac and ½ oz. of borax; the borax will dissolve the shellac, which will be held in suspension; the whole must then be passed through a fine hair sieve, or piece of linen, to rid it of all pieces or impurities. This will keep a very long time, and may be used over and over again.

Great care must be exercised that not too much shellac is used, or the paper will be rendered transparent.

Manipulation.

Dust.—The careful application of india-rubber or bread will generally take away all dust. In using india-rubber, hold the sheet or leaf down by the left hand, and rub gently away from it. If the rubber is used in a to and fro motion, there is great danger of the sheet doubling back and breaking. The bread may be used in a circular motion; and if a book be cleaned from dust by this means without pulling to pieces, all crumbs must be brushed away from the back very carefully before closing the book.

Water stains.—If the stains be from water, the application of boiling water and alum will take them out. This stain is the one most usually found in books, it may be distinguished from other stains by leaving a mark having a sharp edge.

To take such a stain away, pull the book to pieces, strew on the bottom of the pan a handful of powdered alum, on this pour a quantity of boiling water. Immerse each section leaf by leaf in the liquid, and allow to remain for some hours. It may be found rather difficult to get the sheets to go under the water; and as one cannot press them under by hand, on account of the heat, make a substitute by wrapping strips of linen on the end of a piece of wood; keep this handy, it will be found very useful; being round at the end, and soft, it does not tear or go through the paper, as will anything sharp.

The alum water will, after a time, become very discoloured; this is only the stain and other dirt extracted from the paper; throw this away by tipping the dish, or by the use of the syphon; add fresh water, either warm or cold, but preferably warm, to dissolve any excess of alum that may have soaked into the paper, and to further clear it. After a time the whole book may be taken out, placed between pressing boards, and excess of water pressed away by the laying press. The sections are then carefully opened, and hung upon lines or cords stretched across the workshop to dry. When dry, should the paper require it, pass the whole book, section by section, or leaf by leaf, through a size, press, and again hang up to dry. When dry, it will be ready for re-binding. It may happen that only a single leaf is stained; do *not cut* this out as is usually done, but wet a piece of fine string, which lay on the leaf as far in the back as possible; close the book and allow to remain a few minutes; the leaf may then be readily drawn out, the moisture of the string having made the paper soft where it was placed. It may then be cleaned, and when dry and pressed, replaced.

Damp stains may be treated as for water stains, but, as a rule, a book damaged by damp has little or no chance of being made good again. A book so damaged can only be strengthened by re-sizing or some artificial means. To re-size leaves that cannot be plunged into the solution, the sizing may be done with a soft brush. Place the leaf on a piece of glass or marble, and use the brush to the leaf as one would do in pasting; when sized, lift the leaf up very gently and lay it out on paper to dry; when dry, the reverse side is treated in like manner; or a thin paper of a transparent character may be pasted over the pages, either on one or both sides.

Mud.—Luckily a book stained with mud is not of frequent occurrence. Mud seems to be a combination of all that is objectionable, generally it is a mixture of iron and grease. Wash the leaf well in cold water, then in a weak solution of muriatic acid, after which, plunge in a weak solution of chloride of lime. Rinse well, dry, and size. Sometimes it will be necessary to wash the leaf with soap water. Make a soap solution, and gently go over the whole sheet with a soft brush, a shaving brush for instance; this may be done by laying the leaf on a slab of glass: use great care with the brush, or the surface of the paper will be abraised; after which, rinse well with water.

Very often such stains, if fresh, will disappear if a fine jet of water be allowed to play on the parts dirtied, the water being ejected through a fine rose jet.

Fox-marks.—Books so stained may generally be cleaned by immersing the leaves into a weak solution of hydrochloric acid; one must not make the bath too strong, ½ ounce of the acid to 1 pint of water, using the bath hot, will be found about right. Should the marks not give to this treatment, plunge the book, sheet by sheet, into a weak bath of chlorine water. The book may be left in for some hours, taken out and replaced in the hydrochloric bath; after a half hour it may be rinsed with cold water, hung up to dry, and sized.

Finger-marks, commonly called "thumb-marks."—These are the most difficult to erase, the dirt being generally of a greasy nature, and forced into the fibres of the paper. Make a jelly of white or curd soap, apply to the stain, and leave it on for some time, then wash away gently by means of a soft brush *while the leaf is in cold water;* this will, as a rule, take all, or nearly all, away. A slight rinsing in very weak acid water, again with cold water, and when dry size.

Blood stains.—The leaves stained must be plunged into cold water; when thoroughly soaked, the stains may be washed with a soft brush charged with soap, then well rinsed with water again. Dry.

If hot water be used, the heat renders the albumen of the blood insoluble, and the stain will be difficult to erase.

Ink stains (writing).—Some inks are more difficult to erase than others. As a rule ink gives way if the writing be treated with a solution of oxalic acid, and afterwards to a weak solution of chloride of lime. It is perhaps better to immerse the whole leaf in the solution, as the lime is likely to bleach and leave a mark; the leaf should in any case be plunged in warm water afterwards, to wash away the lime and acid, and, after drying, it should be sized.

Ink stains (*marking ink, silver*) may be removed by a solution of tincture of iodine; nitrate of silver, the basis of the ink, is changed into iodide of silver, this is then treated with a solution of cyanide of potassium. It may perhaps be necessary to repeat this two or three times; when quite dissolved out, it must be well washed. As the cyanide is a deadly poison, one may subsitute *hyposulphite of sodium.*

Fat stains.—(1.) Place a piece of blotting-paper on each side of the stain, apply a hot polishing iron very carefully to the paper; this will, in most cases, melt the fat, which will be absorbed by the blotting-paper.

(2.) Scrape pipe clay, or French chalk, which place on the stain, then use the hot iron. The iron must not be used too hot, or the paper will be scorched; a piece of paper should always be placed between the iron and the leaf stained. The powder may be afterwards brushed away.

(3.) May be removed by washing the leaf with ether, or benzoline, placing a pad of blotting-paper under and over the leaf, dabbing the benzoline or ether on the spot with a piece of cotton wool. This process must not be conducted near a flame, both are highly inflammable.

(4.) A mixture of 1 part nitric acid, 10 parts water, is useful in many instances for oil stains. When erased, plunge the whole sheet or leaf into water, changing the water several times. Dry and size.

Ink.—When the writing-paper has been made from inferior rags bleached with excess of chlorine the best ink becomes discoloured.

Reviving old writings.—(1.) Brush the paper over carefully with a solution of sulpho-cyanide of potassium (1 in 20). Then, while still damp, hold over a dish containing hot muriatic acid; the writing will develop deep red.

(2.) Wash the writing with a very weak solution of hydrochloric acid, then carefully apply infusion of galls.

(3.) For letters that have been in sea water, wash with warm water to remove the salt, then soak in weak solution of gallic acid, about 3 grains to the ounce. If this does not make the writing legible enough, wash thoroughly in clean water, and soak in a solution of protosulphate of iron, 10 grains to the ounce.

To restore writing effaced by chlorine.—(1.) Expose the writing to the vapour of sulphuret of ammonia, or dip it into a solution of the sulphuret.

(2.) Ferro-cyanide of potassium, 5 parts.
Water, 85 parts.

Dissolve and immerse the paper in the fluid, then slightly acidulate the solution with sulphuric acid.

Guitaud discovered that sulphuret of ammonia and prussiate of potash revives writing effaced by oxymuriatic acid.

To restore MSS. faded by time.—A moderately concentrated solution of tannin washed over the paper. The MS. to be carefully dried.

To preserve drawings or manuscripts.—Mix with every 100 parts of collodion 2 parts of sterine. Place the paper in question on a perfectly level and even surface, such as a marble table or large slab of glass. Give the paper a thin coat of this collodion, and in about twenty minutes it will be protected by a transparent, brilliant, and imperishable envelope.

To fix drawings or pencil marks.—Pass the paper through a bath of thin size, made either from gelatine or isinglass; or a bath of skim milk.

To render paper waterproof.—Take of borax 100 parts, water 2,250 parts; boil, and while stirring, gradually add powdered shellac 300 parts. When the whole is dissolved, strain through muslin. This will keep a long time and may be bottled.

To render paper incombustible.—Pass the paper through a strong solution of alum, and hang up to dry.

The following, taken from the "English Mechanic," June 19th, 1874, is, I think, of great use to the professional restorer of old books, and will give the binder an idea of what has to be done sometimes :—

"DECIPHERING BURNT DOCUMENTS.

"M. Rathelot, an officer of the Paris Law Courts, has succeeded in an ingenious manner in transcribing a number of the registers which were burnt during the Commune. These registers had remained so long in the fire that each of them seemed to have become a homogeneous block, more like a slab of charcoal than anything else ; and when an attempt was made to detach a leaf it fell away into powder.

"He first cut off the back of the book ; he then steeped the book in water, and afterwards exposed it, all wet as it was, to the heat at the mouth of a warming pipe (*calorifère*). The water as it evaporated raised the leaves one by one, and they could be separated, but with extraordinary precaution. Each sheet was then deciphered and transcribed. The appearance of the pages was very curious—the writing appeared of a dull black, while the paper was of a lustrous black, something like velvet decorations on a black satin ground, so that the entries were not difficult to decipher."

Insects.—A library has generally three kinds of enemies to be guarded against, viz.: insects, dampness, and rats or mice.[1]

Everyone is supposed to know how to guard against dampness and rats or mice. Several means are known how to keep insects at a distance. The first consists in the

[1] Blades, in his "Enemies of Books," includes bookbinders.

proper choice of woods for the book-case: these are cedar, cypress, mahogany, sandal, or very dry and sound oak. All these are compact or of very strong aroma, and are such as insects do not like to pierce. Another source of danger is the use of chemicals in the binding of books.

The insects that make ravages in books multiply very rapidly, and very few libraries are free from them. The microscopic eggs that are left by the female give birth to a small grub, which pierces the leather boards and book for its nourishment, and to get to the air. These are familiarly called bookworms, but by the scientific world they are known as *hypothenemus eruditus* which eats the leather, and *anobium striatum* which bores through the paper. The larvæ of the *dermestes* also attack wood as well as books.

An instance of how these insects were once managed:— M. Fabbroni, Director of the Museum of Florence, who possessed a magnificent library, found, after a year's absence, in the wood and furniture, great havoc made by insects, and his books spoilt by the larvæ, so much so that it gave a fair promise of the total destruction of the whole, unless he could find a method to exterminate the pests. He first painted the holes over with wax, but shortly after he found new worms which killed every particle of wood they touched. He plunged the ordinary wood in arsenic and oil, and other portions he anointed once every month with olive oil, in which he had boiled arsenic, until the colour and odour announced that the solution was perfect. The number then diminished. But a similar method could not be employed for books. M. Fabbroni resolved to anoint the back and sides with aquafortis; in an instant the *dermestes* abandoned their habitation, and wandered to the wood; the oil having evaporized they commenced to develop again, and again began their attacks on the newly bound books. He saw amongst the many spoilt books one remaining intact, and on inquiry found that turpentine had been used in the paste. He then ordered that for the future all paste should be mixed with some such poison. This precaution had the *beneficial* result.

It is not only in Europe that these worms make such ravages in libraries. In the warmer climes they appear to be even more dangerous. And it is a fact that certain libraries are almost a mass of dust, by the books (and valuable ones) falling to pieces. Nearly all authors on this subject agree that the paste which is used is the first cause, or a great help, to all the waste committed by these dangerous *bibliophobes*. Then something must be put into the paste which will resist all these insects and keep them at a distance. The most suitable for this is a mineral salt, such as alum or vitriol; vegetable salts, such as potash, dissolve readily in a moist air and make marks or spots in the books. From experience, it is most desirable to banish everything that may encourage worms, and as it is very rare that persons who occupy themselves with books are not in want of paste, for some repairs or other, either to the bindings or to the books, subjoined is a method of preserving the paste and keeping it moist and free from insects.

Alum, as employed by binders, is not an absolute preservative, although it contributes greatly to the preservation of the leather. Resin as used by shoemakers is preferable, and in effect works in the same way; but oil of turpentine has a greater effect. Anything of strong odour, like aniseed, bergamot, mixed perfectly but in small quantities, preserves the paste during an unlimited time.

Or, make the paste with flour, throw in a small quantity of ground sugar and a portion of *corrosive sublimate*. The sugar makes it pliant and prevents the formation of crust on the top. The sublimate prevents insects and fermentation. This salt does not prevent moisture, but as two or three drops of oil are sufficient to prevent it, all causes of destruction are thus guarded against. This paste exposed to the air hardens without decomposition. If it is kept in an air-tight pot or jar, it will be always ready, without any other preparation.

Books placed in a library should be thoroughly dusted two or three times a year, not only to keep them in all their freshness, but also to prevent any development of insects and to examine for signs of dampness. The interior of a book also asks that care, which unfortunately is neglected very often. After having taken a book from the shelves it should not be opened before ascertaining if the top edge be dusty. If it is a book that has had the edge cut, the dust should be removed with a soft duster, or simply blown off. If it is a book which has uncut edges it should be brushed with rather a hard brush. By this method in opening the volume one need not be afraid that the dirt will enter between the leaves and soil them.

Glue.—The best glue may be known by its paleness, but French glue is now manufactured of inferior quality, made pale by the use of acid, but which on boiling turns almost black. Good glue immersed in water for a day will not dissolve, but swell, while inferior will partly or wholly do so, according to quality.

In preparing glue, a few cakes should be broken into pieces and placed in water for twelve hours, then boiled and turned out into a pan to get cold; when cold, pieces may be cut out and placed in the glue-pot as wanted. This naturally refers to when large quantities are used, but small portions may be boiled in the glue-pot after soaking in water.

Glue loses a great deal of its strength by frequent remelting. It should always be used as hot as possible.

Rice glue or paste.—By mixing rice flour intimately with

cold water, and then gently boiling it, a beautifully white and strong paste is made. It dries almost transparent, and is a most useful paste for fine or delicate work.

Paste.—For ordinary purposes paste consists simply of flour made into a thin cream with water and boiled. It then forms a stiffish mass, which may be diluted with water so as to bring it to any required condition. It is sometimes of advantage to add a little common glue to the paste. Where paste is kept for a long time, various ingredients may be added to prevent souring and moulding. A few cloves form perhaps the best preservative for small quantities; on the larger scale carbolic acid may be used; salicylic acid is also a good preservative, a few grains added to the freshly prepared paste will entirely prevent souring and moulding.

Paste is now made on a commercial scale by various Paste Cos., who send it out to all parts. The paste is exceedingly good, and keeps a long time.

Photographs.—A few words respecting the treatment of photographs may not be out of place here.

To remove a photograph from an old or dirty mount, the surplus of the mount should be cut away; it should then be put into a plate of cold water and be allowed to float off. A little warm water will assist in its coming away more easily, but should it not do so, the photograph has probably been mounted with a solution of india-rubber, and in that case, by holding it near the fire, the rubber will soften, and the print may easily be peeled off.

Very hot water is likely to set up a reaction if the prints were not well washed by the photographer when first sent out.

In mounting photographs, white boards should, as a rule, be avoided, because the colour of the boards is more pure than the lights of the photograph, and deaden the effect. A toned or tinted board is more suitable.

They should be damped, and evenly trimmed and pasted all over with thin best glue or starch, and well rubbed down with a piece of clean paper over the print. If any of the glue or starch oozes out from the sides, it should be wiped off with a clean damp sponge. As photographs lose their gloss in mounting, they must be rolled afterwards in order to restore it. A special machine is used for this.

But it may be wished to introduce the silver print without mounting on a board. To do so, and to keep the print straight, paste a very thin paper on the back, stretching the paper well; this will counteract the pulling power albumen has, and the print will, if this be done properly, remain perfectly straight and not curl up.

Albumen.—Desiccated egg-albumen is now well known in the market in the form of powder. Three teaspoonfuls of cold water added to every $\frac{1}{2}$ teaspoonful of powder represents the normal consistency of egg-albumen.[1]

The manufacture of egg-albumen in the neighbourhood of Moscow is carried on in the houses of the country people. The albumen however is generally roughly prepared and of bad appearance, and often spoils. But egg-albumen is also produced on a manufacturing scale in the neighbourhood of Korotscha, the largest establishment there numbering sixty to seventy workwomen, using about eight million eggs yearly, other establishments using less in proportion.

Albumen is also largely manufactured from blood; 5 oxen or 20 sheep or 34 calves are said to yield the same quantity of dry albumen, viz., 2 lbs. In producing blood-albumen for commerce, the objects borne in mind are the attainment of a substance whose solution is free from colour, possesses coagulation, and which is cheap.

To prevent tools, machines, etc., from rusting.—Boiled linseed oil, if allowed to dry on polished tools, will keep them

[1] See Chapter on Finishing—"Albumen."

from rusting; the oil forms a coat over them which excludes contact from air.

Dissolve $\frac{1}{2}$ oz. of camphor in 1 lb. of lard; take off the scum, and mix as much blacklead as will give the mixture an iron colour. All kinds of machinery, iron or steel, if rubbed over with this mixture, and left on for 24 hours, and then rubbed with a linen cloth, will keep clean for months.

To clean silver mountings.—To restore the colour of tarnished silver clasps, etc., boil the goods, either silver or plated, in enough water to cover them. For every pint of water put into it 2 ounces of carbonate of potash and a $\frac{1}{4}$ lb. of whiting. After boiling them for about a quarter of an hour, clean with a leather, brush, and whiting. They will then look as good as new.

To clean sponges.—Soak the sponge well in diluted muriatic acid for twelve hours. Wash well, then immerse in a solution of hyposulphate of soda to which a few drops of muriatic acid has been added a few moments before. When sufficiently bleached, wash well, and dry in a current of air.

GLOSSARY

OF THE

TECHNICAL TERMS AND IMPLEMENTS USED IN BOOKBINDING.

ALL-ALONG.—When a volume is sewed, and the thread passes from kettle-stitch to kettle-stitch, or from end to end in each sheet, it is said to be sewed "all-along."

ARMING PRESS.—A species of blocking press used by hand; so called from the use of it to impress armorial bearings on the sides of books.

ASTERISK.—A star used by printers at the bottom of the pages meant to supply the places of those cancelled (*see also* CANCEL).

BACKING BOARDS.—Used when backing and for forming the groove. They are made of very hard wood, and sometimes faced with iron; are thicker on the edge intended to form the groove than upon the edge that goes towards the foredge, so that the whole power of the lying press may be directed towards the back.

BACKING HAMMER.—The hammer used for backing and rounding; it has a broad flat face similar to a shoemaker's hammer.

BACKING MACHINE.—A machine for backing cheap work.

BANDS.—The cord whereon the sheets of a volume are sewn. When a book is sewn "flexible" the bands appear upon the back. When the back is sewn so as to imbed the cord in the back, the appearance of raised bands is produced by gluing narrow strips of leather across the back before the volume is covered.

BAND DRIVER.—A blunt chisel used in forwarding, to correct any irregularities in the bands of flexible backs.

BAND NIPPERS.—Flat pincers used for nipping up the band in covering.

BEADING.—The small twist formed when twisting the silk or cotton in head-banding.

BEATING HAMMER.—The heavy short-handled hammer used in beating (generally about 10 lbs.).

BEATING STONE.—The bed on which books are beaten.

BEVELLED BOARDS.—Very heavy boards with bevelled edges; used for antique work.

BLEED.—When a book has been cut down into the print it is said to have been bled.

BLIND-TOOLED.—When a book has been impressed with tools

without being gilt, it is said to be "blind-tooled" or "antique."

BLOCKING PRESS.—Another and more general term for the arming press; one of the chief implements used in cloth work. Used for finishing the side of a cover by a mechanical process.

BLOCKS OR BLOCKING TOOLS.—An engraved stamp used for finishing by means of the blocking press.

BOARDS.—Are of various kinds, each denoting the work it is intended for, such as pressing boards, backing, cutting, burnishing, gilding, etc.

BODKIN.—A strong and short point of steel fixed in a wooden handle, for making the holes through the mill-boards. The slips upon the back of the book are laced through the holes for attaching the mill-board to the book.

BOLE.—A red earthy mineral, resembling clay in character, used in the preparation for gilding edges.

BOLT.—The fold in the head and foredge of the sheets. The iron bar with a screw and nut which secures the knife to the plough.

BOSSES.—Brass or other metal ornamentations fastened upon the boards of books; for ornament or preservation.

BROKEN OVER.—When plates are turned over or folded a short distance from the back edge, before they are placed in the volume, so as to facilitate their being turned easily or laid flat, they are said to be broken over. When a leaf has been turned down the paper is broken.

BURNISH.—The gloss produced by the application of the burnisher to the edges.

BURNISHERS.—Pieces of agate or bloodstone affixed to convenient handles.

CANCELS.—Leaves containing errors which are to be cut out and replaced by corrected pages (*see* ASTERISK).

CAP.—The envelope of paper used to protect the edges while the volume is being covered and finished.

CASE-WORK.—When the cover is made independent of the book, the book being afterwards fastened into it. Refers principally to cloth and bible work.

CATCH-WORD.—A word used and seen in early printed books at the bottom of the page, which word is the first on the following page. To denote the first and last word in an encyclopædia or other book of reference.

CENTRE TOOLS.—Independent tools cut for the ornamentation of the centre of panels and sides.

CLASP.—The hook or catch used for fastening the boards together when the book is closed; used formerly on almost every book.

CLEARING-OUT.—Removing the waste-paper, and paring away any superfluous leather upon the inside, preparatory to pasting down the end-papers.

CLOTH.—Prepared calico, sometimes embossed with different patterns, used for cloth bindings.

COLLATING.—Examining the sheets by the signatures after the volume has been folded, to ascertain if they be in correct sequence.

COMBS.—Instruments with wire teeth used in marbling.

CORNERS.—The triangular tools used in finishing backs and sides. The leather or material covering the corners of half-bound books. The metal ornaments used usually in keeping with clasps.

CROPPED.—When a book has been cut down too much it is said to be cropped.

CUT DOWN.—When a plough-knife dips downward out of the level it is said to "cut down"; on the contrary, if the point is out of the level upwards it is said to "cut up."

CUT UP.—Same as the last explanation.

DIVINITY CALF.—A dark brown calf used generally for religious books, and worked in blind or antique.

DENTELLE.—As the word expresses. A style resembling lace work, finished with very finely cut tools.

DOUBLED.—When in working a tool a second time it is inadvertently not placed exactly in the previous impression, it is said to be "doubled."

EDGE-ROLLED. — When the edges of the boards are rolled, either in blind or in gold.

END-PAPERS. — The papers placed at each end of the volume and pasted down upon the boards.

FILLET.—A cylindrical tool used in finishing, upon which a line or lines are engraved.

FINISHING.—The department that receives the volumes after they are put in leather. The ornaments placed on the volume. The person who works at this branch is termed a finisher.

FINISHING PRESS.—A small press, used for holding books when being finished.

FINISHING STOVE.—A heating box or fire used for warming the various tools used in finishing.

FLEXIBLE.—When a book is sewn on raised bands, and the thread is passed entirely round each band. It is the strongest sewing done at the present time. This term is often misused for limp work, because the boards are limp or flexible.

FOLDER.—A flat piece of bone or ivory used in folding sheets, and in many other manipulations; called also a folding stick. A female engaged in folding sheets.

FOLDING MACHINE.—A machine invented to fold sheets, generally used in newspaper offices.

FOREDGE.—The front edge of a book.

FORWARDING.—The branch that takes the books after they are sewed, and advances them until they are put into leather ready for the finisher. The one who works at this branch is called a forwarder.

FULL-BOUND.—When the sides and back of a volume are covered with leather it is said to be full-bound.

GATHERING. — Collecting the various sheets from piles when folded, so that the arrangement follows the sequence of the signature.

GILT.—Applies to both the edges and to the ornaments in finishing.

GLAIRE.—The white of eggs beaten up.

GOLD CUSHION.—A cushion for cutting the gold leaf on.

GOLD KNIFE.—The knife for cutting the gold; long and quite straight.

GOUGE.—A tool used in finishing; it is a line forming the segment of a circle.

GRAINING BOARDS.—Boards used for producing a grain on calf and russia books. Grain of various form is cut in wood, and by pressure the leather upon which the boards are laid receives the impression.

GRAINING PLATES.—Metal plates same as above.

GUARDS.—Strips of paper inserted in the backs of books intended for the insertion of plates, to prevent the book being uneven when filled; also the strips upon which plates are mounted.

GUIDES.—The groove in which the plough moves upon the face of the cutting press.

GUILLOTINE.—A machine used for cutting paper.

GUINEA-EDGE.—A roll with a pattern similar to the edge of an old guinea.

HALF-BOUND.—When a volume is covered with leather upon the back and corners; and the sides with paper or cloth.

HAND-LETTERS.—Letters fixed in handles; used singly for lettering.

HEAD AND TAIL.—The top and bottom of a book.

HEAD-BAND.—The silk or cotton ornament worked at the head and tail of a volume, as a finish and to make the back even with the boards.

IMPERFECTIONS.—Sheets rejected on account of being in some respect imperfect, and for which others are required to make the work complete.

IN BOARDS.—When a volume is cut after the mill-boards are attached, it is said to be cut in boards.

INSET.—The inner pages of a sheet, cut off in folding certain sizes; to be inset in the centre of the sheet.

JOINTS.—The projection formed in backing to admit the mill-boards. The leather or cloth placed from the projection on to the mill-board is called a joint.

KETTLE-STITCH.—The chain-stitch which the sewer makes at the head and tail of a book. A corruption of either chain-stitch, or catch-up stitch.

KEYS.—Little metal instruments used to secure the bands to the sewing press.

KNOCKING-DOWN IRON.—A piece of iron having a small leg in the centre by which it is secured in the lying press. When fastened there it is used to pound or beat with a hammer the slips into the boards after they are laced in, so that they do not show when the book is covered.

LACED IN.—When the mill-boards are attached to the volume by means of the slips being passed through holes made in the boards, they are said to be laced in or drawn in.

LAW CALF.—Law books are usually bound in calf left wholly uncoloured, hence the term for white calf.

LETTERING BLOCK.—A piece of wood, the upper surface being slightly rounded, upon which side labels are lettered.

LETTERING BOX.—A wooden box in which hand-letters are kept (*see* HAND-LETTERS).

LINING-PAPERS.—The coloured or marbled paper at each end of the volume. Called also end-papers.

MARBLER.—One who marbles the edges of books and paper.

MARBLING.—The art of floating various colours on a size, from which it is transferred to paper or book edges. To stain or vein leather like marble.

MARKING-UP.—When the back of a book is being marked for flexible sewing.

MILL-BOARD.—The boards that are attached to the book. Various kinds are in use now; the most common is made of straw, the best of old naval cordage.

MITRED.—When the lines in finishing meet each other at right angles without overrunning each other, they are said to be mitred. Joined at an angle of 45°.

MUTTON-THUMPING.—A term used in bygone days, indicating the common binding of school books in sheep-skin.

MUTTON-THUMPER.—An old term indicating a bad workman.

OFF-SET.—The impression made by the print against the opposite page, when a book has been rolled or beaten before the ink be dried. (*Also* SET-OFF.)

OUT OF BOARDS.—When a volume is cut before the boards are affixed, it is done out of boards. Nearly the whole of common work is done out of boards.

OUT OF TRUTH.—When a book is not cut square.

OVERCASTING.—An operation in sewing, when the work consists of single leaves or plates. Over-sewing.

PALLET.—The tools used for finishing across backs.

PANEL.—The space between the bands.

PAPERING-UP.—Covering the edges after they are gilt, to protect them while the volume is being covered and finished (*see* CAP).

PARING.—Reducing the edges of the leather by forming a gradual slope.

PARING KNIFE.—The knife used for paring.

PASTE-WASH.—Paste diluted with water.

PEEL.—A wooden instrument used to hang up damp sheets for drying.

PENCIL.—A small brush of camel's hair used for glairing.

PIECED.—Any space that has another leather upon it, as a lettering piece.

PLOUGH.—The instrument used for cutting the edges when the book is in the lying press.

PLOUGH KNIFE.—The knife attached to the plough.

POLISHER.—A steel instrument for giving a gloss to the leather after finishing.

PRESS.—Of various kinds, viz.: lying, cutting, standing, blocking, finishing, etc.

PRESS PIN.—A bar of iron used as a lever for standing presses; a smaller kind for lying presses.

PRESSING BLOCKS.—Blocks of wood used for filling up a standing press when there are not enough books.

PRESSING BOARDS. — Boards used for pressing books between.

PROOF.—The rough edges of certain leaves left uncut by the plough, are "proof" that the book is not cut down (*see also* WITNESS).

RASPED.—The sharp edge taken off mill-boards.

REGISTER.—The ribbon placed in a volume for a marker. A list of signatures attached to the end of early-printed books for the use of the binder. In printing—when on looking through a leaf the print on the recto and verso is not exactly opposite, it is said to be *out of register*.

ROLLING MACHINE.—A machine introduced to save the labour of beating, the sheets being passed between two revolving cylinders.

ROLLS.—Cylindrical ornamental tools used in finishing.

RUNNER. — The front board used in cutting edges.

RUN-UP.—When the back has a fillet run from head to tail without being mitred at each band, it is said to be "run-up."

SAWING-IN.—When the back is sawn for the reception of the cord in sewing.

SAWING MACHINE.—A machine for sawing the backs of books quickly.

SETTING THE HEAD-BAND.—Adjusting the leather in covering so as to form a kind of cap to the head-band.

SEWER.—The person who sews the sheets together on the sewing press—generally a female.

SEWING MACHINE.—A recent invention for the sewing of books with wire and thread.

SHAVING TUB.—The paper cut from the edges of a volume are called shavings. The receptacle into which they fall while the forwarder is cutting is termed the shaving tub.

SHEARS.—Large scissors used for cutting up mill-boards.

SHEEP.—An old term for all common work covered in sheep-skin.

SIGNATURE. — The letter or figure under the footline of the first page of each sheet, to indicate the order of arrangement in the volume.

SIZE.—A preparation used in finishing and gilding, formerly made with vellum, but can now be bought ready for use. When used on paper a thin solution of glue.

SLIPS.—The pieces of twine that project beyond the back of the volume after it is sewn.

SQUARES.—The portions of the boards that project beyond the edges after the book is cut.

STABBING.—The term used formerly for piercing the boards with a bodkin for the slips to pass through; more generally known now as "holeing." The operation of piercing pamphlets for the purpose of stitching.

STABBING MACHINE.—A small machine used for making the holes through the backs of pamphlets.

STANDING PRESS.—A fixed heavy press with a perpendicular screw over the centre.

START.—When any of the leaves are not properly secured in the back, and they project beyond the others, they are said to have started. When the back has been broken by forcing the leaves they start.

STIFFENER.—A thin mill-board used for various purposes.

STITCHING.—The operation of passing the thread through a pamphlet for the purpose of securing the sheets together.

STRAIGHT-EDGE.—A small board having one edge perfectly straight.

STOPS.—Small circular tools, adapted to "stop" a fillet when it intersects at right angles; used to save the time mitring would occupy.

TENON SAW.—A small saw used by bookbinders for sawing the books for sewing. More strictly speaking a carpenter's tool.

TITLE.—The space between the bands upon which the lettering is placed. The leaf in the beginning of a book describing the subject.

TOOLS.—Applied particularly to the hand stamps and tools used in finishing.

TRIMMING.—Shaving the rough edge of the leaves of a book that is not to be cut.

TRINDLE.—A thin strip of wood or iron.

TURNING-UP.—The process of cutting the foredge in such a manner as to throw the round out of the back until the edge is cut. All books that are cut in boards have a pair of trindles thrust between the boards and across the back to assist the operation.

TYING-UP.—The tying of a volume after the cover has been drawn on, so as to make the leather adhere better to the sides of the bands; also for setting the head-band.

TYPE.—Metal letters used in printing and lettering.

TYPE-HOLDER.—An instrument for holding the type when used for lettering.

VARNISH.—Used as a protection to the glaire when polished on the covers of books.

WHIPPING.—Another term for overcasting, but when longer stitches are made.

WITNESS.—When a volume is cut so as to show that it has not been so cut down, but that some of the leaves have still rough edges. These uncut leaves are called "Witness" (*see* PROOF).

WRINKLE.—The uneven surface in a volume, caused by not being properly pressed or by dampness, also caused by improper backing.

INDEX.